Immigration

Other books in the Issues on Trial Series

Affirmative Action

Education

Euthanasia

Free Speech

Gun Control

Homosexuality

Religious Liberty

Women's Rights

Immigration

Mitchell Young, Book Editor

GREENHAVEN PRESS

An imprint of Thomson Gale, a part of The Thomson Corporation

Detroit • New York • San Francisco • New Haven, Conn. • Waterville, Maine • London

THOMSON

™

GALE

Christine Nasso, *Publisher*
Elizabeth Des Chenes, *Managing Editor*

© 2008 The Gale Group.

Star logo is a trademark and Gale and Greenhaven Press are registered trademarks used herein under license.

For more information, contact:
Greenhaven Press
27500 Drake Rd.
Farmington Hills, MI 48331-3535
Or you can visit our Internet site at http://www.gale.com

LIBRARY OF CONGRESS CATALOGING-IN-PUBLICATION DATA

Immigration / Mitchell Young, book editor.
    p. cm. -- (Issues on trial)
    Includes bibliographical references and index.
    ISBN-13: 978-0-7377-3807-0 (hardcover)
    1. Children of immigrants--Legal status, laws, etc.--United States 2. Illegal aliens --Civil rights--United States. 3. Emigration and immigration law--United States. I. Young, Mitchell.
    KF4819.I46 2008
    342.7308'2--dc22

2007037889

ISBN-10: 0-7377-3807-3 (hardcover)

Printed in the United States of America
10 9 8 7 6 5 4 3 2 1

Contents

Foreword   **11**

Introduction   **14**

Chapter 1: Establishing Citizenship Rights for Children of Immigrants

Case Overview *United States v.*   **20**
Wong Kim Ark (1898)

1. The Court's Decision: Children Born   **22**
   in the United States Are Automatically Citizens
   Horace Gray

   Based on English common law and the Fourteenth Amendment, the U.S. Supreme Court rules that children of immigrants born in the United States are automatically granted U.S. citizenship.

2. Dissenting Opinion: Birthright Citizenship   **29**
   Is a Legal Absurdity
   Melville Fuller

   Granting automatic citizenship creates an absurd situation where children of travelers or temporary residents would be granted citizenship. The Fourteenth Amendment, meant to be applied to freed slaves, does not apply to children of immigrants.

3. The *Wong Kim Ark* Case Is a Milestone   **36**
   in Treating All Americans Fairly
   Frank Wu

   By establishing citizenship rights for all people born on U.S. territory, the *Wong Kim Ark* case helped break down unfair barriers for immigrants.

4. The *Wong Kim Ark* Case Ignores   **41**
   Legislative Intent
   P.A. Madison

   In *Wong Kim Ark*, the Supreme Court ignored the legislative history of the Fourteenth Amendment, during which legislators expressly denied that it would grant citizenship to the children of aliens.

5. Immigration Concerns Stir New Controversy   **48**
over the *Wong Kim Ark* Decision
Michael Sandler

Some congressmen have proposed legislation to end "birthright" citizenship, arguing that the *Wong Kim Ark* decision does not apply to the children of illegal aliens.

Chapter 2: Protecting the Civil Rights of the Foreign Born

Case Overview: *United States v.*   **54**
Schneiderman (1943)

1. The Court's Decision: Communist Party   **56**
Membership Does Not Subject a Naturalized
Citizen to Deportation
Frank Murphy

The government cannot retroactively revoke the grant of citizenship simply because an individual joins an unpopular political party.

2. Dissenting Opinion: The Government Has   **64**
the Right to Deport Those It Deems Dangerous
Harlan Fiske Stone

The government should have broad powers to deport aliens and naturalized citizens who subscribe to an ideology enemical to the United States.

3. The *Schneiderman* Case Is Newly Relevant   **70**
in the Age of the War on Terror
Charles H. Hooker

The *Schneiderman* decision may help the government resist pressures to deport aliens and naturalized citizens considered disloyal or dangerous.

4. The Issues of Loyalty Dealt with in   **77**
the *Schneiderman* Case Are Relevant
to Post-9/11 America
David Fontana

Because it dealt with issues that are current today during the War on Terror, such as the real or perceived danger to national security posed by aliens, the *Schneiderman* case has implications for immigration policy in the present.

Chapter 3: Debating Illegal Immigrant Children's Right to Public Education

Case Overview: *Plyler v. Doe* (1982)   **86**

1. The Court's Decision: States Cannot Bar Illegal   **88**
   Immigrant Children from Public Education
   William J. Brennan

   The state has no rational basis to deny education to children who were not legally admitted to the United States.

2. Dissenting Opinion: Denying Free Education   **97**
   to Illegal Aliens Is Not Unconstitutional
   Warren Burger

   While it may be a mistake to deny children in the country illegally the right to an education, it is not the Court's
   job to police social policy by extending the right to an
   education to noncitizens.

3. *Plyler* Is a Watershed Decision for   **105**
   Individual Rights
   Michael A. Olivas

   Good social policy requires that all children be educated,
   whether they are in the United States legally or illegally.

4. *Plyler v. Doe* Was a Blow to Racial Prejudice   **111**
   Alejandra Rincón

   In *Plyler v. Doe* the Court recognized that the fiscal impact of educating undocumented children was small, and
   that in the long run this education was important for the
   nation's future.

5. *Plyler v. Doe* Ignored the Needs of American   **118**
   Taxpayers and Children
   Howard Sutherland

   The court disregarded the costs and impact of including
   illegal alien children in public schools and mistakenly
   took power that rightly belongs to Congress.

Chapter 4: Extending Civil Rights to Undeportable Aliens

Case overview: *Zadvydas v. Davis* (2001)   **126**

1. The Court's Decision: Immigration   **128**
Officials Cannot Detain Undeportable
Criminal Aliens Indefinitely
Stephen Breyer

There must be a time limit to detention and deportation
procedings. If the government cannot show that there is
a likelihood that a criminal aliens will be deported to
their home country, they must be released.

2. Dissenting Opinion: The Court   **136**
Overstepped Its Bounds in Mandating the
Release of Criminal Aliens
Anthony Kennedy

In the 1996 Immigration Responsibility Act, Congress
clearly wanted to prevent the release of criminal aliens
into society. If they cannot be deported, executive agencies have the right to hold them.

3. The *Zadvydas* Decision Allows Potential   **143**
Terrrorists to Live at Large in the United States
Christopher Sheridan

In the post-9/11 era, the *Zadvydas* decision is not only
bad law, it endangers public safety. The decision requires
that suspected terrorists be allowed back on the streets of
America if their home countries will not accept them.

4. Post-9/11 Legislation Has Stymied the Increased   **149**
Rights for Immigrants Promised by *Zadvydas*
N. Alejandra Arroyave

Since 9/11, the new climate of fear has led to legislation—especially the USA Patriot Act— that has expanded
the federal government's ability to detain immigrants.

5. The *Zadvydas* Decision Has Improved   **155**
U.S. Deportation Procedures
Rachel Canty

Immigration and Customs Enforcement has had to dras-
tically alter their procedures as a result of the *Zadvydas*
decision.

Organizations to Contact   **160**

For Further Research   **165**

Index   **170**

Foreword

The U.S. courts have long served as a battleground for the most highly charged and contentious issues of the time. Divisive matters are often brought into the legal system by activists who feel strongly for their cause and demand an official resolution. Indeed, subjects that give rise to intense emotions or involve closely held religious or moral beliefs lay at the heart of the most polemical court rulings in history. One such case was *Brown v. Board of Education* (1954), which ended racial segregation in schools. Prior to *Brown*, the courts had held that blacks could be forced to use separate facilities as long as these facilities were equal to that of whites.

For years many groups had opposed segregation based on religious, moral, and legal grounds. Educators produced heartfelt testimony that segregated schooling greatly disadvantaged black children. They noted that in comparison to whites, blacks received a substandard education in deplorable conditions. Religious leaders such as Martin Luther King Jr. preached that the harsh treatment of blacks was immoral and unjust. Many involved in civil rights law, such as Thurgood Marshall, called for equal protection of all people under the law, as their study of the Constitution had indicated that segregation was illegal and un-American. Whatever their motivation for ending the practice, and despite the threats they received from segregationists, these ardent activists remained unwavering in their cause.

Those fighting against the integration of schools were mainly white southerners who did not believe that whites and blacks should intermingle. Blacks were subordinate to whites, they maintained, and society had to resist any attempt to break down strict color lines. Some white southerners charged that segregated schooling was *not* hindering blacks' education. For example, Virginia attorney general J. Lindsay Almond as-

serted, "With the help and the sympathy and the love and respect of the white people of the South, the colored man has
risen under that educational process to a place of eminence
and respect throughout the nation. It has served him well." So
when the Supreme Court ruled against the segregationists in
Brown, the South responded with vociferous cries of protest.
Even government leaders criticized the decision. The governor
of Arkansas, Orval Faubus, stated that he would not "be a
party to any attempt to force acceptance of change to which
the people are so overwhelmingly opposed." Indeed, resistance
to integration was so great that when black students arrived at
the formerly all-white Central High School in Arkansas, federal troops had to be dispatched to quell a threatening mob of
protesters.

Nevertheless, the *Brown* decision was enforced and the
South integrated its schools. In this instance, the Court, while
not settling the issue to everyone's satisfaction, functioned as
an instrument of progress by forcing a major social change.
Historian David Halberstam observes that the *Brown* ruling
"deprived segregationist practices of their moral legitimacy. . . .
It was therefore perhaps the single most important moment
of the decade, the moment that separated the old order from
the new and helped create the tumultuous era just arriving."
Considered one of the most important victories for civil rights,
Brown paved the way for challenges to racial segregation in
many areas, including on public buses and in restaurants.

In examining *Brown*, it becomes apparent that the courts
play an influential role—and face an arduous challenge—in
shaping the debate over emotionally charged social issues.
Judges must balance competing interests, keeping in mind the
high stakes and intense emotions on both sides. As exempli-
fied by *Brown*, judicial decisions often upset the status quo
and initiate significant changes in society. Greenhaven Press's
Issues on Trial series captures the controversy surrounding influential court rulings and explores the social ramifications of

such decisions from varying perspectives. Each anthology highlights one social issue—such as the death penalty, students' rights, or wartime civil liberties. Each volume then focuses on key historical and contemporary court cases that helped mold the issue as we know it today. The books include a compendium of primary sources—court rulings, dissents, and immediate reactions to the rulings—as well as secondary sources from experts in the field, people involved in the cases, legal analysts, and other commentators opining on the implications and legacy of the chosen cases. An annotated table of contents, an in-depth introduction, and prefaces that overview each case all provide context as readers delve into the topic at hand. To help students fully probe the subject, each volume contains book and periodical bibliographies, a comprehensive index, and a list of organizations to contact. With these features, the Issues on Trial series offers a well-rounded perspective on the courts' role in framing society's thorniest, most impassioned debates.

Introduction

Immigration has recently been in the news. The United States is experiencing an unprecedented wave of legal immigrants coming to live in the country. In addition, an estimated 12–20 million illegal immigrants reside in the country, adding to controversy over current immigration policy. While Americans have considered their country a "nation of immigrants," issues such as population growth, competition for jobs, and ability to assimilate the newcomers have once again brought controversy over immigration into focus. Moreover, worries about security after the terrorist attacks of September 11, 2001 (9/11), have renewed old controversies about loyalty and the need to keep the country secure from those who would do America harm.

None of these controversies is new—indeed many have been addressed by past U.S. Supreme Court decisions. Two decisions in particular stand out as relevant to today's controversies, *United States v. Wong Kim Ark* (1894) and *United States v. Schneiderman* (1943). The first case has implications for the status of children born in the United States to illegal immigrants. The second deals with dissent against the U.S. government and its governing principles by naturalized immigrants; it is relevant in an era when some Muslim immigrants are under scrutiny because of participation in Islamic organizations or donations to pro-Islamic charities. Both of these Supreme Court decisions remain in effect today, and both have profound consequences for immigration policy.

In the *Wong Kim Ark* case, the Court ruled that children born in U.S. territory automatically became citizens, regardless of whether the parents were eligible for citizenship. (At the time?? Chinese were not able to become U.S. citizens.) The ruling was based on the Fourteenth Amendment's clause that "all persons born in the United States, and subject to the jurisdiction thereof, are citizens of the United States." The immediate effect of the decision was to grant citizenship to all American-born children.

Nevertheless, with the large number of illegal immigrants in the country today (Wong Kim Ark's parents were in the country legally), birthright citizenship has come under scrutiny. According to James R. Edwards Jr. of the Center for Immigration Studies, the Supreme Court's decision rewards those who are in the country illegally simply for having a child here, "immigration authorities are highly unlikely to try to deport an illegal alien whose child is an American citizen. Therefore, 'birthright citizenship' provides illegal aliens an 'anchor baby' who provides relative assurance of permanent residence, if not legal status." Moreover, the *Wong Kim Ark* decision can be seen as undermining democracy. "Granting birthright citizenship to the U.S.-born children of illegal aliens undermines the process by which the American people and their representatives have sought to design and enforce the country's immigration, naturalization, and citizenship laws," according to Charles Wood, former Counsel to the U.S. Senate Judiciary Committee's Subcommittee on Immigration.

Those in favor of birthright citizenship believe the Constitution is unambiguously on their side. "Birthright citizenship is a constitutional right no less for the children of undocumented persons than for descendants of passengers of the *Mayflower*," according to attorney and former Supreme Court law clerk James C. Ho. Immigrants' rights supporters believe that any attempt to change the law, aside from being unconstitutional, would punish children for the acts of their parents. Moreover, they point out that "having an American-born baby is no easy ticket to government entitlements. Illegal aliens who give birth to children in the USA can still be deported, and should an American-born child wish to sponsor his parents, he must wait 21 years before he can do so," according to Raul Reyes, a New York lawyer.

Opponents of birthright counter that the Fourteenth Amendment states that those born in the United States must also be "subject to the jurisdiction thereof" to receive automatic citizenship. If illegal immigrants are outside the jurisdiction of the United States, they and any children born here should not receive birthright citizenship. The question of the exact meaning of jurisdiction could be an opening for the Supreme Court's decision in *Wong Kim Ark* to be reversed. Congress might also become involved in the issue as "based on the intent of the framers of the Fourteenth Amendment, some believe that Congress could exercise its . . . powers to prevent the children of illegal aliens from automatically becoming citizens of the United States," notes political science professor Edward Erler. Nevertheless, "an effort [to revoke birthright citizenship] in 1997 failed in the face of intense political opposition from immigrant rights groups." It seems likely that with increased political attention to immigration, legal and illegal, this issue will be revisited in the future.

While *Wong Kim Ark* was about who was eligible for citizenship, *Schneiderman v. United States* dealt with the civil rights of those already granted citizenship. William Schneiderman came to the United States as a child in the first decade of the 1900s, and as a young man became deeply involved in work with the Communist Party. He applied for and was granted American citizenship in the 1920s. More than a decade later the U.S. government tried to revoke his citizenship and have him deported. The government claimed that his efforts on behalf of communism showed him to be disloyal to the Constitution and the general principles of American society. The Court ruled that political criticism, even of a radical nature, was protected by the Constitution for native-born Americans and naturalized citizens alike and thus Schneiderman's citizenship could not be revoked.

The *Schneiderman* case was all but forgotten until the events of 9/11 put national attention on the connection between immigration and national security. In the 1930s—the era of the *Schneiderman* case—communists were seen as a threat to America's safety. In the post-9/11 world, Muslims, particularly Islamic activists, are seen as a threat. Immigrants' rights groups point to the case of Sami al-Arian, a University of South Florida professor and supporter of Palestinian rights. Al-Arian was accused by the government of raising money for a group called Palestinian Islamic Jihad and tried under anti-terrorism laws. He was found not guilty of most charges, but agreed to plead guilty to an additional charge in order to, according to his supporters, spare his family the ordeal of another trial. He will serve a prison sentence and then be deported.

Al-Arian is not a citizen, and as such, was eligible to be deported. He is, however, a long-term resident of the United States, with American-born children. Civil rights groups worry that his case could set the stage for an attack on the rights of naturalized citizens to criticize the government. Professor John Esposito, an expert on Islam at Georgetown University, believes that the media ignore:

> the thousands of Muslims indiscriminately arrested, detained, monitored and interviewed and not found guilty or released for lack of evidence; the number of Islamic charities shut down but despite the passage of years not successfully prosecuted; the continued detention of Muslims like Prof. Sami al-Arian, whose jury verdict as well as the post-trial agreement forged by Justice Department and Defense attorneys were ignored by the trial judge.

It may be that in the near future, a new case will come before the Supreme Court that will pit the rights of a naturalized citizen who the government is trying to deport for his or her advocacy of radical Islam. If that happens, the *Schneiderman* decision will be a key precedent that the justices will have to consult, even if they eventually choose to overturn it.

Despite the general view that America is a "nation of immigrants," immigration has always had its controversial aspects. Supreme Court decisions have had a major impact on how the nation treats newcomers. In *Issues on Trial: Immigration* judges, lawyers, and commentators present their views on some of the most important cases affecting immigration. Along with *United States v. Wong Kim Ark* and *United States v. Schneiderman*, this volume contains debates over *Plyler v. Doe*, which granted the right to free public schooling to illegal immigrant children, and *Zadvydas v. Davis*, which ended indefinite detention of criminal aliens. Taken together, the cases show that virtually all areas of immigration law are controversial, sometimes even more than a hundred years after the Supreme Court has ruled on an issue.

CHAPTER 1

Establishing Citizenship Rights for Children of Immigrants

Case Overview

United States v. Wong Kim Ark (1898)

Wong Kim Ark was born to Chinese parents in San Francisco in 1873. At the time, Chinese were not allowed to become U.S. citizens, and so his parents had remained subjects of the Chinese emperor despite their long residence in the United States. In 1890 Wong went on an extended visit to his parents' homeland, while they remained in San Francisco.

In August 1895 Wong Kim Ark attempted to return to the United States, but he was refused permission to enter the country. The United States had passed a series of laws, the Chinese Exclusion Acts, which sharply reduced Chinese immigration, allowing only teachers, scholars and a few other categories of professionals to settle here. As Wong was a laborer, he was excluded from the country and held in custody. He, however, claimed he was an American citizen, as he was born in the United States.

Wong and his lawyers claimed that under the Fourteenth Amendment he was granted citizenship simply by being born in the country. The relevant part of the amendment reads: "All persons born or naturalized in the United States, and subject to the jurisdiction thereof, are citizens of the United States and of the state wherein they reside." The district courts in California disagreed with this argument, and his lawyers appealed the case to the U.S. Supreme Court.

The Court agreed with Wong. In his decision, Justice Horace Gray gives a long overview of the concept of American citizenship, starting with its roots in English common law. According to Gray, the tradition that all persons born in England were subject to, and owed loyalty to, the king had been brought to the English colonies in America. When these became independent, the tradition continued, with citizenship being granted at birth and loyalty to the American government being expected. Gray makes these arguments because of the clause "subject to the jurisdiction" thereof, in the Fourteenth Amendment—the government lawyers seeking to exclude Wong held that as subjects of the Chinese emperor, Wong's parents were not within the full jurisdiction of the United States, and that he inherited this status from them at his birth.

Gray's ruling in favor of Wong still stands. It means that any child born in the United States instantly becomes a citizen. This has recently become a matter of controversy in the debate over illegal immigration. Opponents of so-called birthright citizenship argue that granting citizenship to children born to illegal aliens rewards those who have broken U.S. laws and makes enforcement of immigration restrictions difficult. Indeed Justice Melville Fuller foresaw this difficulty in his dissent in *Wong*; he noted that the ruling would lead to separation of families if some members were deported while the U.S.-born children were permitted to remain because of their "birthbright." Those fighting birthright citizenship claim that *Wong* may not apply to children of illegal aliens, because the concept of being in the country illegally had not been invented at the time of the decision. In addition, they believe this right can be taken away by legislation, as the Fourteenth Amendment, on which Gray's decision was based, grants Congress the right to enforce its provisions.

The Court's Decision: Children Born in the United States Are Automatically Citizens

Horace Gray

Horace Gray was an associate justice of the U.S. Supreme Court from 1882 to 1902. In this opinion, Justice Gray relies on English common law as well as the Fourteenth Amendment to conclude that, with few exceptions, all children born in the United States are automatically American citizens. Under the English system, all those born in the king's realm owed him their allegiance and were subject to his laws. Likewise, according to Gray everyone—with the exception of children of diplomats—born in the United States is subject to American law and thus, by the plain words of the Fourteenth Amendment, are citizens automatically.

The question presented by the record is whether a child born in the United States, of parents of Chinese descent, who at the time of his birth are subjects of the emperor of China, but have a permanent domicile and residence in the United States, and are there carrying on business, and are not employed in any diplomatic or official capacity under the emperor of China, becomes at the time of his birth a citizen of

Horace Gray, majority opinion, *United States v. Wong Kim Ark*, March 28, 1898.

the United States, by virtue of the first clause of the fourteenth amendment of the constitution: 'All persons born or
naturalized in the United States, and subject to the jurisdiction thereof, are citizens of the United States and of the state
wherein they reside. . . . '

The Constitution Is Silent on Citizenship

The constitution of the United States, as originally adopted,
uses the words 'citizen of the United States' and 'natural-born
citizen of the United States.' By the original constitution, every
representative in congress is required to have been 'seven years
a citizen of the United States,' and every senator to have been
'nine years a citizen of the United States,' and 'no person except a natural-born citizen, or a citizen of the United States at
the time of the adoption of this constitution, shall be eligible
to the office of president.' The fourteenth article of amendment, besides declaring that 'all persons born or naturalized in
the United States, and subject to the jurisdiction thereof, are
citizens of the United States and of the state wherein they
reside,' also declares that 'no state shall make or enforce any
law which shall abridge the privileges or immunities of citizens of the United States; nor shall any state deprive any person of life, liberty, or property, without due process of law,
nor deny to any person within its jurisdiction the equal protection of the laws.' And the fifteenth article of amendment
declares that 'the right of citizens of the United States to vote
shall not be denied or abridged by the United States, or by
any state, on account of race, color, or previous condition of
servitude.'

The constitution nowhere defines the meaning of these
words, either by way of inclusion or of exclusion, except in so
far as this is done by the affirmative declaration that 'all persons born or naturalized in the United States, and subject to
the jurisdiction thereof, are citizens of the United States.' In
this, as in other respects, it must be interpreted in the light of

the common law, the principles and history of which were familiarly known to the framers of the constitution. The language of the constitution, as has been well said, could not be understood without reference to the common law. In *Minor v. Happersett*, Chief Justice [Morrison] Waite, when construing, in behalf of the court, the very provision of the fourteenth amendment now in question, said: 'The constitution does not, in words, say who shall be natural-born citizens. Resort must be had elsewhere to ascertain that.' And he proceeded to resort to the common law as an aid in the construction of this provision. . . .

Citizenship Law Based on English Common Law

The fundamental principle of the common law with regard to English nationality was birth within the allegiance—also called 'ligealty,' 'obedience,' 'faith,' or 'power'—of the king. The principle embraced all persons born within the king's allegiance, and subject to his protection. Such allegiance and protection were mutual . . . and were not restricted to natural-born subjects and naturalized subjects, or to those who had taken an oath of allegiance; but were predicable of aliens in amity, so long as they were within the kingdom. Children, born in England, of such aliens, were therefore natural-born subjects. But the children, born within the realm, of foreign ambassadors, or the children of alien enemies, born during and within their hostile occupation of part of the king's dominions, were not natural-born subjects, because not born within the allegiance, the obedience, or the power, or, as would be said at this day, within the jurisdiction, of the king. . . .

It thus clearly appears that by the law of England for the last three centuries, beginning before the settlement of this country, and continuing to the present day, aliens, while residing in the dominions possessed by the crown of England, were within the allegiance, the obedience, the faith or loyalty, the protection, the power, and the jurisdiction of the English sovereign; and therefore every child born in England of alien parents was a natural-born subject, unless the child of an ambassador or other diplomatic agent of a foreign state, or of an alien enemy in hostile occupation of the place where the child was born.

The same rule was in force in all the English colonies upon this continent down to the time of the Declaration of Independence, and in the United States afterwards, and continued to prevail under the constitution as originally established. . . .

The Importance of the Fourteenth Amendment

The first section of the fourteenth amendment of the constitution begins with the words, 'All persons born or naturalized in the United States, and subject to the jurisdiction thereof, are citizens of the United States and of the state wherein they reside.' As appears upon the face of the amendment, as well as from the history of the times, this was not intended to impose any new restrictions upon citizenship, or to prevent any persons from becoming citizens by the fact of birth within the United States, who would thereby have become citizens according to the law existing before its adoption. It is declaratory in form, and enabling and extending in effect. Its main purpose doubtless was, as has been often recognized by this court, to establish the citizenship of free negroes, which had been denied in the opinion delivered by Chief Justice [Roger Taney] in *Scott v. Sanford* (1857) and to put it beyond doubt that all blacks, as well as whites, born or naturalized within the jurisdiction of the United States, are citizens of the United States. But the opening words, 'All persons born,' are general, not to say universal, restricted only by place and jurisdiction, and not by color or race. . . .

Limited Exceptions to Citizenship at Birth

The fourteenth amendment affirms the ancient and fundamental rule of citizenship by birth within the territory, in the allegiance and under the protection of the country, including all children here born of resident aliens, with the exceptions or qualifications (as old as the rule itself) of children of foreign sovereigns or their ministers, or born on foreign public ships, or of enemies within and during a hostile occupation of part of our territory, and with the single additional exception of children of members of the Indian tribes owing direct allegiance to their several tribes. The amendment, in clear words and in manifest intent, includes the children born within the territory of the United States of all other persons, of whatever race or color, domiciled within the United States. Every citizen or subject of another country, while domiciled here, is within the allegiance and the protection, and consequently subject to the jurisdiction, of the United States. His allegiance to the United States is direct and immediate, and, although but local and temporary, continuing only so long as he remains within our territory, is yet, in the words of Lord [English jurist Edward] Coke in Calvin's Case, 'strong enough to make a natural subject, for, if he hath issue here, that issue is a natural-born subject'; and his child, as said by [lawyer] Mr. [Horace] Binney in his essay before quoted, 'If born in the country, is as much a citizen as the natural-born child of a citizen, and by operation of the same principle. . . .'

To hold that the fourteenth amendment of the constitution excludes from citizenship the children born in the United States of citizens or subjects of other countries, would be to deny citizenship to thousands of persons of English, Scotch, Irish, German, or other European parentage, who have always been considered and treated as citizens of the United States.

Whatever considerations, in the absence of a controlling provision of the constitution, might influence the legislative or the executive branch of the government to decline to admit persons of the Chinese race to the status of citizens of the United States, there are none that can constrain or permit the judiciary to refuse to give full effect to the peremptory and explicit language of the fourteenth amendment, which declares and ordains that 'all persons born or naturalized in the United States, and subject to the jurisdiction thereof, are citizens of the United States. . . .'

Two Sources of Citizenship

The fourteenth amendment of the constitution, in the declaration that 'all persons born or naturalized in the United States, and subject to the jurisdiction thereof, are citizens of the United States and of the state wherein they reside,' contemplates two sources of citizenship, and two only—birth and naturalization. Citizenship by naturalization can only be acquired by naturalization under the authority and in the forms of law. But citizenship by birth is established by the mere fact of birth under the circumstances defined in the constitution. Every person born in the United States, and subject to the jurisdiction thereof, becomes at once a citizen of the United States, and needs no naturalization. A person born out of the jurisdiction of the United States can only become a citizen by being naturalized, either by treaty, as in the case of the annexation or foreign territory, or by authority of congress, exercised either by declaring certain classes of persons to be citizens, as in the enactments conferring citizenship upon foreign-born children of citizens, or by enabling foreigners individually to become citizens by proceedings in the judicial tribunals, as in the ordinary provisions of the naturalization acts. . . .

No one doubts that the amendment, as soon as it was promulgated, applied to persons of African descent born in the United States, wherever the birthplace of their parents might have been; and yet, for two years afterwards, there was no statute authorizing persons of that race to be naturalized. If the omission or the refusal of congress to permit certain classes of persons to be made citizens by naturalization could be allowed the effect of correspondingly restricting the classes of persons who should become citizens by birth, it would be in the power of congress, at any time, by striking negroes out of the naturalization laws, and limiting those laws, as they were formerly limited, to white persons only, to defeat the main purpose of the constitutional amendment.

The fact, therefore, that acts of congress or treaties have not permitted Chinese persons born out of this country to become citizens by naturalization, cannot exclude Chinese persons born in this country from the operation of the broad and clear words of the constitution: 'All persons born in the United States, and subject to the jurisdiction thereof, are citizens of the United States. . . .'

The evident intention, and the necessary effect, of the submission of this case to the decision of the court upon the facts agreed by the parties, were to present for determination the single question, stated at the beginning of this opinion, namely, whether a child born in the United States, of parents of Chinese descent, who, at the time of his birth, are subjects of the emperor of China, but have a permanent domicile and residence in the United States, and are there carrying on business, and are not employed in any diplomatic or official capacity under the emperor of China, becomes at the time of his birth a citizen of the United States. For the reasons above stated, this court is of opinion that the question must be answered in the affirmative.

> *"If children born in the United States were deemed presumptively and generally citizens, this was not so when they were born of aliens whose residence was merely temporary."*

Dissenting Opinion: Birthright Citizenship Is a Legal Absurdity

Melville Fuller

In the dissenting opinion in United States v. Wong Kim Ark, *Chief Justice Melville Fuller holds that the Fourteenth Amendment does not automatically grant citizenship to all persons born within U.S. territory. Rather, such persons must be fully subject to U.S. jurisdiction, and not born of parents who are subject to another nation's law. At the time Chinese law prohibited the emperor's subjects from renouncing their nationality and American law prohibited Chinese in America from naturalizing. Thus, the Chinese are not fully subject to U.S. jurisdiction and children born to Chinese parents, such as Wong Kim Ark, should not be granted automatic citizenship at birth. Fuller was Chief Justice of the United States from 1888 to 1910.*

To be 'completely subject' to the political jurisdiction of the United States is to be in no respect or degree subject to the political jurisdiction of any other government.

Chinese Law Forbids Changing Nationality

Now, I take it that the children of aliens, whose parents have not only not renounced their allegiance to their native coun-

Melville Fuller, dissenting opinion, *United States v. Wong Kim Ark*, March 28, 1898.

try, but are forbidden by its system of government, as well as by its positive laws, from doing so, and are not permitted to acquire another citizenship by the laws of the country into which they come, must necessarily remain themselves subject to the same sovereignty as their parents, and cannot, in the nature of things, be, any more than their parents, completely subject to the jurisdiction of such other country.

Generally speaking, I understand the subjects of the emperor of China—that ancient empire, with its history of thousands of years, and its unbroken continuity in belief, traditions, and government, in spite of revolutions and changes of dynasty—to be bound to him by every conception of duty and by every principle of their religion, of which filial piety is the first and greatest commandment; and formerly, perhaps still, their penal laws denounced the severest penalties on those who renounced their country and allegiance, and their abettors, and, in effect, held the relatives at home of Chinese in foreign lands as hostages for their loyalty. And, whatever concession may have been made by treaty in the direction of admitting the right of expatriation in some sense, they seem in the United States to have remained pilgrims and sojourners as all their fathers were. At all events, they have never been allowed by our laws to acquire our nationality, and, except in sporadic instances, do not appear ever to have desired to do so.

The fourteenth amendment was not designed to accord citizenship to persons so situated, and to cut off the legislative power from dealing with the subject.

Citizenship Is a Precious Heritage

The right of a nation to expel or deport foreigners who have not been naturalized or taken any steps towards becoming citizens of a country is as absolute and unqualified as the right to prohibit and prevent their entrance into the county.

But can the persons expelled be subjected to 'cruel and unusual punishments' in the process of expulsion, as would be the case if children born to them in this country were separated from them on their departure, because citizens of the United States? Was it intended by this amendment to tear up parental relations by the roots?

The fifteenth amendment provides that 'the right of citizens of the United States to vote shall not be denied or abridged by the United States or by any state on account of race, color or previous condition of servitude.' Was it intended thereby that children of aliens should, by virtue of being born in the United States, be entitled, on attaining majority, to vote, irrespective of the treaties and laws of the United States in regard to such aliens?

In providing that persons born or naturalized in the United States, and subject to the jurisdiction thereof, are citizens, the fourteenth amendment undoubtedly had particular reference to securing citizenship to the members of the colored race, whose servile status had been obliterated by the thirteenth amendment, and who had been born in the United States, but were not, and never had been, subject to any foreign power. They were not aliens (and, even if they could be so regarded, this operated as a collective naturalization), and their political status could not be affected by any change of the laws for the naturalization of individuals.

Nobody can deny that the question of citizenship in a nation is of the most vital importance. It is a precious heritage, as well as an inestimable acquisition; and I cannot think that any safeguard surrounding it was intended to be thrown down by the amendment. . . .

Children Born to Temporary Residents Are Not Citizens

These considerations lead to the conclusion that the rule in respect of citizenship of the United States prior to the fourteenth amendment differed from the English common-law rule in vital particulars, and, among others, in that it did not recognize allegiance as indelible, and in that it did recognize an essential difference between birth during temporary and birth during permanent residence. If children born in the United States were deemed presumptively and generally citizens, this was not so when they were born of aliens whose residence was merely temporary, either in fact or in point of law.

Did the fourteenth amendment impose the original English common-law rule as a rigid rule on this country?

Did the amendment operate to abridge the treaty-making power, or the power to establish a uniform rule of naturalization?

I insist that it cannot be maintained that this government is unable, through the action of the president, concurred in by the senate, to make a treaty with a foreign government providing that the subjects of that government, although allowed to enter the United States, shall not be made citizens thereof, and that their children shall not become such citizens by reason of being born therein.

A treaty couched in those precise terms would not be incompatible with the fourteenth amendment, unless it be held that that amendment has abridged the treaty-making power.

Chinese Are Not Completely Subject to Our Laws

Nor would a naturalization law excepting persons of a certain race and their children be invalid, unless the amendment has abridged the power of naturalization. This cannot apply to our colored fellow citizens, who never were aliens, were never beyond the jurisdiction of the United States.

'Born United States, and subject to the jurisdiction thereof,' and 'naturalized in the United States, and subject to the jurisdiction thereof,' mean born or naturalized under such circumstances as to be completely subject to that jurisdiction—that is, as completely as citizens of the United States who are, of course, not subject to any foreign power, and can of right claim the exercise of the power of the United States on their behalf wherever they may be. When, then, children are born the United States to the subjects of a foreign power, with which it is agreed by treaty that they shall not be naturalized thereby, and as to whom our own law forbids them to be naturalized, such children are not born so subject to the jurisdiction as to become citizens, and entitled on that ground to the interposition of our government, if they happen to be found in the country of their parents' origin and allegiance, or any other.

Immigration Is Governed by Treaty

Turning to the treaty between the United States and China, concluded July 28, 1868, the ratifications of which were exchanged November 23, 1869, and the proclamation made February 5, 1870, we find that by its sixth article it was provided: 'Citizens of the United States Visiting or residing in China shall enjoy the same privileges, immunities, or exemptions in respect of travel or residence as may there be enjoyed by the citizens or subjects of the most favored nation. And, reciprocally Chinese subjects residing in the United States, shall enjoy the same privileges, immunities, and exemptions in respect to travel or residence as may there be enjoyed by the citizens or subjects of the most favored nation. But nothing herein contained shall be held to confer naturalization on the citizens of the United States in China, nor upon the subjects of China in the United States.'

It is true that in the fifth article the inherent right of man to change his home or allegiance was recognized, as well as 'the mutual advantage of the free migration and emigration of their citizens and subjects, respectively, from the one country to the other, for the purposes of curiosity, of traffic, or as permanent residents.'

All this, however, had reference to an entirely voluntary emigration for these purposes, and did not involve an admission of change of allegiance unless both countries assented, but the contrary, according to the sixth article.

By the convention of March 17, 1894, it was agreed 'that Chinese laborers or Chinese of any other class, either permanently or temporarily residing within the United States, shall have for the protection of their persons and property all rights that are given by the laws of the United States to citizens of the most favored nation, excepting the right to become naturalized citizens.'

These treaties show that neither government desired such change, nor assented thereto. Indeed, if the naturalization laws of the United States had provided for the naturalization of Chinese persons, China manifestly would not have been obliged to recognize that her subjects had changed their allegiance thereby. But our laws do not so provide, and, on the contrary, are in entire harmony with the treaties.

Ineligible for Citizenship

I think it follows that the children of Chinese born in this country do not, ipso facto, become citizens of the United States unless the fourteenth amendment overrides both treaty and statute. Does it bear that construction; or, rather, is it not the proper construction that all persons born in the United States of parents permanently residing here, and susceptible of becoming citizens, and not prevented therefrom by treaty or statute, are citizens, and not otherwise?

But the Chinese, under their form of government, the treaties and statutes, cannot become citizens nor acquire a permanent home here, no matter what the length of their stay may be.

In *Fong Yue Ting v. U.S.*, it was said, in respect of the treaty of 1868: 'After some years' experience under that treaty, the government of the United States was brought to the opinion that the presence within our territory of large numbers of Chinese laborers, of a distinct race and religion, remaining strangers in the land, residing apart by themselves, tenaciously adhering to the customs and usages of their own country, unfamiliar with our institutions, and apparently incapable of assimilating with our people, might endanger good order, and be injurious to the public interests; and therefore requested and obtained from China a modification of the treaty.'

It is not to be admitted that the children of persons so situated become citizens by the accident of birth. On the contrary, I am opinion that the president and senate by treaty, and the congress by legislation, have the power, notwithstanding the fourteenth amendment, to prescribe that all persons of a particular race, or their children, cannot become citizens, and that it results that the consent to allow such persons, to come into and reside within our geographical limits does not carry with it the imposition of citizenship upon children born to them while in this country under such consent, in spite of treaty and statute.

In other words, the fourteenth amendment does not exclude from citizenship by birth children born in the United States of parents permanently located therein, and who might themselves become citizens; nor, on the other hand, does it arbitrarily make citizens of children born in the United States of parents who, according to the will of their native government and of this government, are and must remain aliens.

Tested by this rule, Wong Kim Ark never became and is not a citizen of the United States, and the order of the district court should be reversed.

> *"Abolishing birthright citizenship would reinforce a caste system and inherited privilege: an individual would be bound by the status of her parents."*

The *Wong Kim Ark* Case Is a Milestone in Treating All Americans Fairly

Frank Wu

In this article, Dean Frank H. Wu of the Wayne State University law school argues that the Wong Kim Ark *decision, which held that all persons born on U.S. territory are automatically citizens, is a major safeguard for all Americans, not just Asian Americans. According to Wu, the decision ensures that those born in America are not bound by the status of their parents, thus helping America live up to its ideals. The author also expresses concern that today, when immigration is a hotly debated issue, the birthright citizenship established by Wong Kim Ark's challenge to U.S. law is now in jeopardy.*

Like most Americans, I have almost always taken my citizenship for granted. But like some Americans, I have had my citizenship challenged often enough to realize that I should care about its origins. Although I have always tried to assimilate as much as possible and could hardly have done otherwise, I have from time to time been disappointed that the efforts to conform are not enough for those who define membership in our democracy on the basis of race rather than principle.

I was born a citizen, but birth alone did not always confer citizenship. All of us who care about our civil rights should realize that we owe a measure of our shared equality to an individual named Wong Kim Ark.

In the 1920s, the Supreme Court confirmed that Japanese and Asian Indians were not "free white persons" and thus could not naturalize.

More than a century ago in California, Wong took on the federal government in an effort to win his right to remain in his homeland. His legal case ended up in the Supreme Court. His victory shows how, despite recurring prejudice, our country can remain true to its ideals. It is worthwhile to reflect on our history, not to condemn the past by contemporary standards, but to understand how we came to where we are now. There are valuable lessons in these forgotten episodes.

In the middle of the nineteenth century, Chinese immigrants began to arrive here. They were recruited to work on Southern plantations as well as Eastern factories. On Southern plantations, they were touted as replacements for freed slaves. In Eastern factories, they were used as strikebreakers as unions based on ethnicity were starting to form. Famously, more than ten thousand of them helped build the transcontinental railroad. When they finished the job, they were not allowed to join the celebration at Promontory Point, Utah. Afterward, they were fired.

Remarkably, however, it was during the period of Chinese Exclusion that birthright citizenship emerged as a constitutional doctrine. In frontier towns such as San Francisco, Chinese laborers represented more than a quarter of the population. With an economic downturn, whites—many, of whom themselves were recent arrivals to the United States—saw non-whites as competition in racial terms. Politicians began to agitate against them, shouting the rallying cry, "The Chinese Must Go!" Even progressive leaders such as Samuel Gompers, founder of the American Federation of Labor, argued that it was "meat or rice," suggesting that Caucasians could not succeed against Asians and had no choice but to limit their entry.

In 1882, heeding warnings that Asians might overwhelm the West Coast or make it racially mixed, Congress passed the Chinese Exclusion Act. As the name of the bill suggested, it prohibited most people of Chinese descent from coming to this country with only limited exceptions. Later, Congress would extend the policy to create an Asiatic Barred Zone. In the 1920s, the Supreme Court confirmed that Japanese and Asian Indians were not "free white persons" and thus could not naturalize.

I believe that birthright citizenship guarantees our most basic right, to remain in the land of our origin. It signals both that we belong to the nation and that the nation belongs to us.

After Exclusion, contrary to images of a submissive subculture isolated from the mainstream, Chinese communities engaged in civil disobedience in the best traditions of American liberty. Chinese who were already present when Exclusion passed were allowed to stay. They could sponsor their children as immigrants under an exception to the act. So they brought in "paper sons," men who claimed falsely to be their descendants. Chinese communities also organized themselves to protest their exclusion through politics and lawsuits. The *Wong* case was only one example.

Wong Kim Ark had sued to be re-admitted to the birthplace, after taking a trip to China. He argued that by virtue of his birth on its soil he was a citizen of the United States, even though his parents were racially barred from achieving that status.

In opposing Wong, the federal government argued in its court briefs, "There certainly should be some honor and dignity in American citizenship that would be scarred from the foul and corrupting taint of a debasing alienage." The Solicitor General asked, "Are Chinese children born in this country to share with the descendants of the patriots of the American Revolution to exalted qualification of being eligible to the Presidency of the nation?" He answered, "If so, then verily there has been a most degenerate departure from the patriotic ideals of our forefathers; and surely in that case American citizenship is not worth having."

Rejecting these racial arguments, the Court based its ruling on the Fourteenth Amendment. That provision of the Constitution is familiar as the source of "equal protection of the laws." The Court gave a literal interpretation to its opening lines, that "all persons born or naturalized in the United States, and subject to the jurisdiction thereof, are citizens of the United States and of the State wherein they reside." By doing so, the Supreme Court united racial minority groups. For the Fourteenth Amendment had been passed to overturn the notorious 1857 Supreme Court decision in the *Dred Scott* case, which declared that blacks were not citizens. Thus, because African Americans were citizens, Asian immigrants could be citizens as well—and, vice versa.

Abolishing birthright citizenship would ensure inherited privilege: an individual would be bound by the status of their parents.

Today's debate over birthright citizenship brings the connection full circle. Opponents of birthright citizenship have focused on Latino immigrants. They have said that Mexican women wait until they are about to go into labor, and then cross the border to have American children, supposedly to gain government entitlements. This spectacular racial stereotype is the symbolic sister to the "welfare queen" in the Eighties—the African American single woman who has children solely to obtain public benefits.

With anxieties about immigration, some demagogues have renewed calls for a racial vision of United States citizenship. They [are] forthright in their claim that this is a white, Anglo-Saxon Protestant nation by heritage. Other writers have tried to pit communities of color against one another, suggesting that African Americans should oppose immigration, and immigrants should oppose affirmative action. Yet African Americans, Asian Americans, Latinos, and everyone else should see through Wong Kim Ark that the citizenship status we enjoy depends on the citizenship of others. Abolishing birthright citizenship would reinforce a caste system and inherited privilege: an individual would be bound by the status of her parents and those whose ancestors arrived earlier would have a stronger claim to the nation.

I believe that birthright citizenship guarantees our most basic right, to remain as equals in the land founded for liberty. The law signals both that we belong to the nation and that the nation belongs to us.

"[Taking] into account both the legislative and language history behind the citizenship clause . . . leaves the Wong Kim Ark *ruling as worthless as a three-dollar bill."*

The *Wong Kim Ark* Case Ignores Legislative Intent

P.A. Madison

In the following piece, P.A. Madison argues that the Wong Kim Ark *case was incorrectly decided. Relying both on the legislative history of the Fourteenth Amendment and its predecessor, the Civil Rights Bill of 1866, Madison argues that the framers of the amendment meant to include only those subject to the "complete" jurisdiction of the United States. Complete jurisdiction implied, in the language of the nineteenth century, not only being subjects to laws, but also having allegiance to the country. That means that children travelers and others temporarily in the country, especially those retaining citizenship to other nations, are not to be granted automatic citizenship. Madison is a former congressional researcher who writes on a variety of political and legal issues.*

There is a misconception floating around that suggests the ruling in *U.S. v. Wong Kim Ark* is the definite guiding rule of interpretation over the fourteenth amendment's citizenship clause. Worst, some even go as far to suggest *Wong Kim Ark* is settled law. Nothing could be further from the truth.

P.A. Madison, "Why the *Wong Kim Ark* Case Can Never Be Settled Law," *Federalist Blog*, December 10, 2006. Reproduced by permission of the author.

Obscure Colonial Law

Reading the majorities opinion in [*Wong*] *Kim Ark*, one can't help but wonder why so much emphasis is being placed on such obscure and irrelevant historical overviews as colonial and foreign law. With two previous established court decisions that substantially covered the same ground regarding the meaning and application of the words found in the fourteenth amendments citizenship clause, leaves one to wonder what is going on here?

Deeper into the decision, justice Horace Gray (writing for the majority) reveals exactly what the majority is up to: They are attempting to avoid discussion over the construction of the clause by the two Senators whom are most responsible for its language found in the Constitution, Jacob M. Howard and Lyman Trumbull.

It is clear the *Wong Kim Ark* majority recognized the fact that the only viable approach to the conclusion they sought was to somehow distant themselves from the recorded history left behind by the citizenship clause framers. Justice Gray made no attempt to hide this fact when he wrote: "Doubtless, the intention of the congress which framed, and of the states which adopted, this amendment of the constitution, *must be sought in the words of the amendment, and the debates in congress are not admissible as evidence to control the meaning of those words.*"

Justice John Paul Stevens would take issue with this inept attempt by the majority to rewrite the Constitution: "*A refusal to consider reliable evidence of original intent in the Constitution is no more excusable than a judge's refusal to consider legislative intent.*"

No Concern for Original Intent

The *Wong Kim Ark* court was refusing to look at both the original intent and legislative construction behind the words because they knew it would be fatal to their pre-determined intent of reversing what Congress had inserted into the US Constitution. So they set out to avoid [The Fourteenth Amendment's Framers] Howard and Trumbull like the plague.

Reviewing what both Sen. Howard, who was responsible for the drafting of the citizenship clause, and Sen. Trumbull, clearly declared what was the intended effect of the language of the clause; [leaving] little doubt to why justice Gray desired to avoid the legislative history and previous court rulings on the effect of this language.

The first major hurdle Howard presents to the *Wong Kim Ark* majority is that he specifically declared the clause to be "virtue of natural law and national law." Perhaps this is why Gray wasted much of his commentary along common law themes. National law posed too large of a hurdle to dismiss outright—national law only recognized citizenship by birth to those who were not subject to some other foreign power.

Howard then goes on to introduce the clause as to specifically excluding all "persons born in the United States who are foreigners, aliens," and persons "who belong to the families of ambassadors or foreign ministers accredited to the Government of the United States, but will include every other class of persons." [The] only class of persons the clause can operate on is American citizens (natural law), regardless of their race—which is exactly what was intended.

More Evidence Against the *Wong Kim Ark* Decision

To make matters even worst for the court, Howard goes on to say in May of 1868 that the "Constitution as now amended, forever withholds the right of citizenship in the case of accidental birth of a child belonging to foreign parents within the limits of the country."

Lyman Trumbull goes on to present an insurmountable barrier of his own by declaring: "The provision is, that 'all persons born in the United States, and subject to the jurisdiction thereof, are citizens.' That means 'subject to the complete jurisdiction thereof.' What do we mean by 'complete jurisdiction thereof?' *Not owing allegiance to anybody else.* That is what it means."

Sen. Howard follows up by stating that: "the word 'jurisdiction,' as here employed, ought to be construed so as to imply a full and complete jurisdiction on the part of the United States, whether exercised by Congress, by the executive, or by the judicial department; that is to say, the same jurisdiction in extent and quality as applies to every citizen of the United States now."

Howard then goes on to declare, "Certainly, gentlemen cannot contend that an Indian belonging to a tribe, although born within the limits of a State, is subject to this full and complete jurisdiction."

Do illegal aliens or visitors enjoy the same quality of jurisdiction as a citizen of the United States? Can an alien be tried for Treason against the United States? Here Sen. Howard makes it impossible for "subject to the jurisdiction" to operate on anyone other than American citizens.

John A. Bingham, chief architect of the 14th amendment's first section, considered the proposed national law on citizenship as "simply declaratory of what is written in the Constitution, that every human being born within the jurisdiction of the United States of parents not owing allegiance to any foreign sovereignty is, in the language of your Constitution itself, a natural born citizen. . . ."

Previous Court Decisions Do Not Support Birthright Citizenship

As mentioned earlier, the Supreme Court had already tackled the meaning of the 14th amendment's citizenship clause prior to *Wong Kim Ark*, and unlike the [*Wong*] *Kim Ark* court, did consider the intent and meaning of the words by those who debated the language of the clause. In the *Slaughterhouse* cases the court noted that "[t]he phrase, 'subject to its jurisdiction' was intended to exclude from its operation children of ministers, consuls, and citizens or subjects of foreign States born within the United States."

Even the dissenting minority affirmed that the result of the citizenship clause was designed to ensure that all persons born within the United States were both citizens of the United States and the state in which they resided, provided they were not at the time subjects of any foreign power.

The court in *Elk v. Wilkins* (1884) correctly determined that "subject to the jurisdiction" of the United States required "not merely subject in some respect or degree to the jurisdiction of the United States, but completely subject to their political jurisdiction, and owing them direct and immediate allegiance." Both Jacob Howard and Lyman Trumbull affirm this.

America's own naturalization laws from the very beginning never recognized children born to aliens to be anything other than aliens if the parents had not declared their allegiance to the United States—a sure sign that the framers never adopted the unconditional jus soli rule. Instead, children under national law followed the condition of their father until he had become naturalized.

A Worthless Ruling

When all is said and done, the majority in *Wong Kim Ark* reveals their true nonsensical position: "To hold that the fourteenth amendment of the constitution excludes from citizenship the children born in the United States of citizens or subjects of other countries, would be to deny citizenship to thousands of persons of English, Scotch, Irish, German, or other European parentage, who have always been considered and treated as citizens of the United States."

Well now, there was no question at issue involving citizenship being withheld on account of the 14th amendment to American citizens, and had the court bothered to consider the history of the amendment, they would have easily discovered it is all about granting citizenship to American citizens regardless of their race. The idea of withholding citizenship upon birth to subjects of other countries within the limits of this country was, well, the desired result of declaring who is, and who isn't, a citizen of the United States.

The court in *Minor vs. Happersett* (1874) acknowledged that some, not all, but some authorities go as far to "include as citizens children born within the jurisdiction without reference to the citizenship of their parents. As to this class there have been doubts, but never as to the first [born to American citizens]."

It was these kind of doubts Howard desired to settle through constitutional amendment. Sen. Howard said of the amendment: "It settles the great question of citizenship and removes all doubt as to what persons are or are not citizens of the United States."

To add additional insult, the court says: "Nor can it be doubted that it is the inherent right of every independent nation to determine for itself, and according to its own constitution and laws, what classes of persons shall be entitled to its citizenship." Yet, the court refused to recognize the fact the United States had done just that through its revised statutes and Constitution.

The most significant truth to come out of the entire *Wong Kim Ark* ruling was from chief justice [Melville] Fuller himself, when he said, "the words 'subject to the jurisdiction thereof,' in the amendment, were used as synonymous with the words 'and not subject to any foreign power.'" He was absolutely correct. . . .

[The] only reason the language of the fourteenth differs from the civil rights bill of 1866, which used the language "and not subject to any foreign power, excluding Indians not taxed" to restrict citizenship, is because Sen. Howard feared a State could begin taxing Indians, thereby making them eligible for citizenship. Because Indians, and other classes of foreigners whom Congress and the States desired to withhold citizenship from, owed allegiance to a foreign power (Indian tribes were considered independent nations), the fourteenth would become just as restrictive against Indians by demanding full jurisdiction on part of the United States as with any other class of foreigners.

[Taking] into account both the legislative and language history behind the citizenship clause—and the courts own stated objective in reaching the conclusion they did while also taking into account two prior Supreme Court holdings—leaves the Wong Kim Ark ruling as worthless as a three-dollar bill. *Slaughterhouse* and *Elk* still stand as the only controlling case law that is fully supported by the history and language behind the citizenship clause as found in the first section of the 14th amendment.

> *"Someday relatively soon the question of birthright citizenship may reach the Supreme Court."*

Immigration Concerns Stir New Controversy over the *Wong Kim Ark* Decision

Michael Sandler

Michael Sandler is a staff reporter for Congressional Quarterly. *In this article, Sandler notes the emerging controversy over "birthright" citizenship in America, a legal precedent that was confirmed by the* Wong Kim Ark *decision. Some congressional representatives have proposed legislation that would end birthright citizenship for the children of illegal immigrants, claiming the practice creates an incentive for people to come to the United States illegally. The legislation would likely face a legal challenge at the Supreme Court level; while the* Wong Kim Ark *ruling seems to indicate that such legislation would be unconsitutional, jurists and legal scholars have indicated there might be room to modify or overrule that ruling.*

"**A**ll persons born or naturalized in the United States and subject to the jurisdiction thereof are citizens of the United States."

Those words, the first sentence of the 14th Amendment, embody a birthright that millions of Americans have enjoyed. At one point during Supreme Court Justice Samuel A. Alito

Michael Sandler, "Toward a More Perfect Definition of 'Citizen,'" *Congressional Quarterly*, February 13, 2006, p. 388, published by CQ Press, a division of Congressional Quarterly Inc. Copyright © 2006 by Congressional Quarterly Inc. All rights reserved. Reproduced by permission.

Jr.'s Senate confirmation hearings [in January 2006], New York Democrat Charles E. Schumer pressed him on whether he agreed that the sentence was a "fairly clear and straightforward provision of the Constitution."

Not an Easy Legal Question

"All persons means all persons," Schumer said encouragingly. "That's pretty easy."

It was not easy enough for Alito to answer on the spot, however. "It may turn out to be a very simple question; it may turn out to be a complicated question," he said. "I would have to go through the whole judicial decision-making process before reaching a conclusion."

Simple or not, Schumer's question—whether those words would prevent Congress from passing a law denying citizenship to someone born on U.S. soil—lies at the heart of an intensely emotional debate. For now, it is on the periphery of congressional consideration of illegal immigration, but someday relatively soon the question of birthright citizenship may reach the Supreme Court.

That outcome would suit Republican [Representative] Nathan Deal of Georgia just fine. Deal, leader of an effort in Congress to bar the children of illegal immigrants from receiving automatic citizenship, says the language in the 14th Amendment is murky and has been misinterpreted over the years. Furthermore, he says, the words of the amendment have been a magnet for immigrants who enter the country illegally, have "anchor babies," then claim that deportation would cruelly separate them from their family.

A Question of Jurisdiction

The Supreme Court has never directly addressed the ambiguities in the Constitution that are seen by Deal and others who want to limit the 14th Amendment's scope. That creates an opening for Congress to restrict birthright citizenship—and then let the courts decide whether that limit is constitutional. In Deal's view, the phrase "subject to the jurisdiction thereof" is ambiguous enough that it might exclude children of parents who are foreign nationals. Automatic citizenship is now granted to anyone born in the United States, even the children of tourists.

Opponents say Deal and his supporters—his legislation had 83 cosponsors as of last week—are overreaching. All immigrants, legal or not, are subject to the jurisdiction of U.S. laws, says California's Howard L. Berman, the No. 2 Democrat on the House Judiciary Committee. Furthermore, Berman says he is baffled at conservative Republicans, who normally insist on a textual reading of the Constitution, building a case that the court must "interpret" the 14th Amendment. "The fact that the court has not had reason to explore this is because Congress has not had the inclination to adopt something that is so contrary to the plain meaning of those words," he said.

Active Legal Disputes

Schumer had used much the same argument in framing his questions to Alito. "President [George W.] Bush has stated his beliefs that judges should be strict constructionists, rigidly adhering to the letter of the Constitution," he told the judge. But Alito refused to be drawn in. "There are active legal disputes about the meaning of that provision at this time," he said.

For now, the debate is academic. Republican leaders prevented Deal's measure from being considered in December as a proposed amendment to an already contentious border security bill, which went on to be passed by the House. But even if he had been successful, his legislation would have to pass an even more skeptical Senate, where leading Republicans call the effort "futile."

But with public discontent over illegal immigration growing, Deal believes he has a case and a chance. "I think any vehicle that would get the issue before the Supreme Court is the right vehicle," he said.

An Ambiguous Amendment

Should that day come, Deal and others would look for guidance to John C. Eastman, a constitutional law professor at Chapman University in Orange, Calif., and director of the Center for Constitutional Jurisprudence at the conservative Claremont Institute.

Eastman testified before a House Judiciary subcommittee in September that the Constitution's citizenship clause has been misinterpreted for more than a century.

Eastman has zeroed in on what the 1866 Civil Rights Act—a statutory forerunner of the 14th Amendment, which was added to the Constitution two years later—said about citizenship. Drafted to guarantee citizenship to recently freed slaves, the law was more direct in who was eligible: "All persons born in the United States, and not subject to any foreign power, excluding Indians not taxed, are hereby declared to be citizens of the United States." The 14th Amendment employed the more ambiguous clause "subject to the jurisdiction thereof," instead of "not subject to any foreign power."

This leaves little doubt in Eastman's mind that Congress understood a clear distinction between "basic territorial jurisdiction" such as traffic laws, and "complete jurisdiction," which encompasses a person's allegiance to a nation.

The Supreme Court confirmed his assessment in *Elk v. Wilkins*, an 1884 ruling that rejected a citizenship claim by John Elk, an American Indian who was born on a reservation but subsequently moved off, and therefore was denied his right to vote.

The *Wong Kim Ark* Decision and Illegal Immigration

But Eastman said the court "misread" the citizenship clause 14 years later in *United States v. Wong Kim Ark*. Wong Kim Ark was born in the United States to Chinese parents. After a visit to China, he was denied readmission to the United States. An

1882 law denied birthright citizenship to the [descendants] of Chinese nationals, and the government claimed that those children would be subject to the rule of its emperor. But the court ruled that common law and the 14th Amendment guaranteed citizenship to all persons born in the United States, regardless of their ethnic heritage.

Jack M. Balkin, a constitutional law professor at Yale University, said that even though the original understanding of the amendment may be ambiguous, the *Wong Kim* decision offered clarity.

"Now the question is 'what if Congress passes a law that says children of illegal immigrants are not citizens?'" he asked. "*Wong Kim Ark* seems to suggest the statute would be unconstitutional. But you could distinguish that it does not specifically involve illegal aliens."

What the court would do, however, is difficult to predict, Balkin said, particularly since it has two new members and virtually no modern case law about the issue to rely on.

"We should not assume it's an easy case," Balkin said. He suspects the court would "tilt" toward striking down Deal's bill if it became law. However, "it's not a slam-dunk either way."

CHAPTER 2

Protecting the Civil Rights of the Foreign Born

Case Overview

United States v. Schneiderman (1943)

In the late 1930s war was threatening to break out in Europe. Two totalitarian philosophies, communism and fascism, were confronting each other on that continent. In America adherents of both ideologies were using discontent over the economy, which was just beginning to recover from the Great Depression, to gain recruits. It was in this atmosphere that federal authorities brought a case to strip William Schneiderman, a Russian-born immigrant, of his citizenship. The government was most likely trying to send a signal that extremist activities would not be tolerated in the United States; it got a court decision that affirmed the right to political activities, however extreme.

Schneiderman had grown up poor. At an early age he was attracted to the communist message of equality and justice for the working class. He became heavily involved in activities with the Communist Party in the United States, serving in educational and leadership roles. Having been born in Russia and brought to the United States at an early age, he was not a citizen. He applied for and was granted citizenship in 1927. In 1939, in the tense political atmosphere described above, the government sought to rescind his citizenship, making the case that his radical beliefs showed that he was not "attached to the principles of United States constitution" as required by the naturalization laws. In addition, the government claimed that by saying he was attached to constitutional principles, Schneiderman had committed fraud in his citizenship application.

The Supreme Court majority disagreed with the government. Following the argument of Schneiderman's lawyer, the politician Wendell Willkie, they held that as the Constitution itself places virtually no limit on how it can be amended or changed, that advocacy of radical political positions did not show disloyalty to constitutional principles. Essentially any political argument was fair game, protected by the Constitution's guarantee of free speech. In addition, the Court worried that, by using denaturalization as a tool to ensure loyalty among immigrant citizens, the government would be creating a two-tier system, whereby the native born were able to exercise their free speech rights more fully than naturalized citizens.

Today, in the climate of the War on Terror, the *Schneiderman* case has been rediscovered. Naturalized citizens of Islamic background have come under suspicion for ties to various religion organizations. The 1943 decision in *Schneiderman* provides a strong protection for these individuals, requiring that the government show "clear and convincing" proof of disloyal activity, rather than mere advocacy of ideas, in order to have them stripped of their citizenship.

> *"The constitutional fathers, fresh from a revolution, did not forge a political strait-jacket for the generations to come."*

The Court's Decision: Communist Party Membership Does Not Subject a Naturalized Citizen to Deportation

Frank Murphy

Frank Murphy was a politician before he was appointed to the Supreme Court by Franklin Roosevelt. Murphy served on the Court from 1940 to 1949. In this decision, Justice Murphy holds that the United States cannot deport William Schneiderman for involvement with the Communist Party. Schneiderman has always behaved peacefully, so the only reason for deportation is his political activities. Murphy, however, believes that respecting the principles of the U.S. Constitution, as is required of naturalized citizens, is consistent with expressing dissent against the Constitution. Freedom of speech is a primary value of the Constitution, and it would be ridiculous to hold that exercising free speech rights does not respect the Constitution.

The question is whether the naturalization of petitioner, an admitted member of the Communist Party of the United States, was properly set aside by the courts below some twelve years after it was granted. We agree with our brethren of the minority that our relations with Russia, as well as our views

Frank Murphy, majority opinion, *United States v. Schneiderman*, 320 U.S. 118, June 21, 1943.

regarding its government and the merits of Communism are immaterial to a decision of this case. Our concern is with what Congress meant by certain statutes and whether the Government has proved its case under them.

While it is our high duty to carry out the will of Congress in the performance of this duty we should have a jealous regard for the rights of petitioner. We should let our judgment be guided so far as the law permits by the spirit of freedom and tolerance in which our nation was founded, and by a desire to secure the blessings of liberty in thought and action to all those upon whom the right of American citizenship has been conferred by statute, as well as to the native born. And we certainly should presume that Congress was motivated by these lofty principles.

We are directly concerned only with the rights of this petitioner and the circumstances surrounding his naturalization, but we should not overlook the fact that we are a heterogeneous people. In some of our larger cities a majority of the school children are the offspring of parents only one generation, if that far, removed from the steerage of the immigrant ship, children of those who sought refuge in the new world from the cruelty and oppression of the old, where men have been burned at the stake, imprisoned, and driven into exile in countless numbers for their political and religious beliefs. Here they have hoped to achieve a political status as citizens in a free world in which men are privileged to think and act and speak according to their convictions, without fear of punishment or further exile so long as they keep the peace and obey the law.

This proceeding was begun on June 30, 1939, . . . to cancel petitioner's certificate of citizenship granted in 1927. This section gives the United States the right and the duty to set aside and cancel certificates of citizenship on the ground of 'fraud' or on the ground that they were 'illegally procured.' The complaint charged that the certificate had been illegally procured in that petitioner was not, at the time of his naturalization, and during the five years proceding his naturalization 'had not behaved as, a person attached to the principles of the Constitution of the United States and well disposed to the good order and happiness of the United States, but in truth and in fact during all of said times, respondent (petitioner) was a member of and affiliated with and believed in and supported the principles of certain organizations then known as the Workers (Communist) Party of America and the Young Workers (Communist) League of America, whose principles were opposed to the principles of the Constitution of the United States and advised, advocated and taught the overthrow of the Government, Constitution and laws of the United States by force and violence.' The complaint also charged frandulent procurement in that petitioner concealed his Communist affiliation from the naturalization court. The Government proceeds here not upon the charge of fraud but upon the charge of illegal procurement. . . .

Schneiderman's Background

Certain facts are undisputed. Petitioner came to this country from Russia in 1907 or 1908 when he was approximately three. In 1922, at the age of sixteen, he became a charter member of the Young Workers (now Communist) League in Los Angeles and remained a member until 1929 or 1930. In 1924, at the age of eighteen, he filed his declaration of intention to become a citizen. Later in the same year or early in 1925 he became a member of the Workers Party, the predecessor of the Communist Party of the United States. That membership has continued to the present. His petition for naturalization was filed on January 18, 1927, and his certificate of citizenship was issued on June 10, 1927, by the United States District Court for the Southern District of California. He had not been arrested or subjected to censure prior to 1927 and there is nothing in the record indicating that he was ever connected with any overt illegal or violent action or with any disturbance of any sort.

For its case the United States called petitioner, one Humphreys, a former member of the Communist Party, and one Hynes, a Los Angeles police officer formerly in charge of the radical squad, as witnesses, and introduced in evidence a number of documents. Petitioner testified on his own behalf, introduced some documentary evidence, and read into the record transcripts of the testimony of two university, professors given in another proceeding.

Petitioner testified to the following: As a boy he lived in Los Angeles in poverty stricken circumstances and joined the Young Workers League to study what the principles of Communism had to say about the conditions of society. He considered his membership and activities in the League and the Party during the five-year period between the ages of sixteen and twenty-one before he was naturalized, as an attempt to investigate and study the causes and reasons behind social and economic conditions. Meanwhile he was working his way through night high school and college. From 1922 to about 1925 he was 'educational director' of the League. The duties of this non-salaried position were to organize classes, open to the public, for the study of Marxist theory, to register students and to send out notices for meetings; petitioner did no teaching. During 1925 and 1926 he was corresponding secretary of the Party in Los Angeles; this was a clerical, not an executive position. In 1928 he became an organizer or official spokesman for the League. His first executive position with the Party came in 1930 when he was made an organizational secretary first in California, then in Connecticut and later in Minnesota where he was the Communist Party candidate for governor in 1932. Since 1934 he has been a member of the Party's National Committee. At present he is secretary of the Party in California. . . .

Naturalization Is a Privilege

The Constitution authorizes Congress 'to establish an uniform Rule of Naturalization,' and we may assume that naturalization is a privilege, to be given or withheld on such conditions as Congress sees fit. But because of our firmly rooted tradition of freedom of belief, we certainly will not presume in construing the naturalization and denaturalization acts that Congress meant to circumscribe liberty of political thought by general phrases in those statutes. As Chief Justice [Charles E.] Hughes said in dissent in the *Macintosh* case, such general phrases 'should be construed, not in opposition to, but in accord with, the theory and practice of our Government in relation to freedom of conscience.'

When petitioner was naturalized in 1927, the applicable statutes did not proscribe Communist beliefs or affiliation as such. They did forbid the naturalization of disbelievers in organized government or members of organizations teaching such disbelief. Polygamists and advocates of political assassination were also barred. Applicants for citizenship were required to take an oath to support the Constitution, to bear true faith and allegiance to the same and the laws of the United States, and to renounce all allegiance to any foreign prince, potentate, state or sovereignty. And, it was to 'be made to appear to the satisfaction of the court' of naturalization that immediately preceding the application, the applicant 'has resided continuously within the United States five years at least, ... and that during that time he has behaved as a man of good moral character, attached to the principles of the Constitution of the United States, and well disposed to the good order and happiness of the same.' Whether petitioner satisfied this last requirement is the crucial issue in this case.

To apply the statutory requirement of attachment correctly to the proof adduced, it is necessary to ascertain its meaning. On its face the statutory criterion is not attachment to the Constitution, but behavior for a period of five years as a man attached to its principles and well disposed to the good order and happiness of the United States. Since the normal connotation of behavior is conduct, there is something to be said for the proposition that the 1906 Act created a purely objective qualification, limiting inquiry to an applicant's previous conduct. If this objective standard is the requirement, petitioner satisfied the statute. His conduct has been law abiding in al respects. According to the record he has never been arrested, or connected with any disorder, and not a single written or spoken statement of his, during the relevant period from 1922 to 1927 or thereafter, advocating violent overthrow of the Government, or indeed even a statement apart from his testimony in this proceeding, that he desired any change in the Constitution has been produced. The sole possible criticism is petitioner's membership and activity in the League and the Party, but those memberships qua memberships, were immaterial under the 1906 Act. In *United States v. Schwimmer*, and *United States v. Macintosh*, however, it was held that the statute created a test of belief-that an applicant under the 1906 Act must not only behave as a man attached to the principles of the Constitution, but must be so attached in fact at the time of naturalization. We do not stop to reexamine this construction for even if it is accepted the result is not changed. As mentioned before, we agree with the statement of Chief Justice Hughes in dissent in *Macintosh*'s case that the behavior requirement is 'a general phrase which should be construed, not in opposition to, but in accord with, the theory and practice of our government in relation to freedom of conscience. . . .'

The claim that petitioner was not in fact attached to the Constitution and well disposed to the good order and happiness of the United States at the time of his naturalization and for the previous five year period is twofold: First, that he believed in such sweeping changes in the Constitution that he simply could not be attached to it; Second, that he believed in and advocated the overthrow by force and violence of the Government, Constitution and laws of the United States.

In support of its position that petitioner was not in fact attached to the principles of the Constitution because of his membership in the League and the Party, the Government has directed our attention first to petitioner's testimony that he subscribed to the principles of those organizations, and then to certain alleged Party principles and statements by Party Leaders which are said to be fundamentally at variance with the principles of the Constitution. At this point it is appropriate to mention what will be more fully developed later—that under our traditions beliefs are personal and not a matter of mere association, and that men in adhering to a political party or other organization notoriously do not subscribe unqualifiedly to all of its platforms or asserted principles. Said to be among those Communist principles in 1927 are: the abolition of private property without compensation; the erection of a new proletarian state upon the ruins of the old bourgeois state; the creation of a dictatorship of the proletariat; of denial of political rights to others than members of the Party or of the proletariat; and the creation of a world union of soviet republics. Statements that American democracy 'is a fraud' and that the purposes of the Party are 'utterly antagonistic to the purposes for which the American democracy, so called, was formed, are stressed.

Freedom of Thought is Guaranteed

Those principles and views are not generally accepted—in fact they are distasteful to most of us—and they call for considerable change in our present form of government and society. But we do not think the government has carried its burden of proving by evidence which does not leave the issue in doubt that petitioner was not in fact attached to the principles of the Constitution and well disposed to the good order and happiness of the United States when he was naturalized in 1927.

The constitutional fathers, fresh from a revolution, did not forge a political strait-jacket for the generations to come. Instead they wrote Article V [of the Constitution] and the First Amendment, guaranteeing freedom of thought, soon followed. Article V contains procedural provisions for constitutional change by amendment without any present limitation whatsoever except that no State may be deprived of equal representation in the Senate without its consent. This provision and the many important and far-reaching changes made in the Constitution since 1787 refute the idea that attachment to any particular provision or provisions is essential, or that one who advocates radical changes is necessarily not attached to the Constitution. As Justice [Oliver Wendell] Holmes said, 'Surely it cannot show lack of attachment to the principles of the Constitution that (one) thinks that it can be improved.' Criticism of, and the sincerity of desires to improve the Constitution should not be judged by conformity to prevailing thought because, 'if there is any principle of the Constitution that more imperatively calls for attachment than any other it is the principle of free thought—not free thought for those who agree with us but freedom for the thought that we hate.' Whatever attitude we may individually hold toward persons and organizations that believe in or advocate extensive changes in our existing order, it should be our desire and concern at all times to uphold the right of free discussion and free thinking to which we as a people claim primary attachment. To neglect this duty in a proceeding in which we are called upon to judge whether a particular individual has failed to manifest attachment to the Constitution would be ironical indeed.

> "What could be more important in the
> selection of citizens of the United States
> than that the prospective citizen be at-
> tached to the principles of the Consti-
> tution?"

Dissenting Opinion: The Government Has the Right to Deport Those It Deems Dangerous

Harlan Fiske Stone

Chief Justice Harlan Fiske Stone served on the Supreme Court from 1925 to 1946, during the last five years of which he was chief justice. In his dissenting opinion, Chief Justice Stone defers to Congress, holding that the legislation regarding naturalized citizens clearly states that those who do not respect the principles of the U.S. Constitution may be deported. He then goes on to find that the principles of the Communist Party do not respect the Constitution. Moreover, William Schneiderman was not only an ardent adherent of communist ideas, but a propagandist for the cause. It is preposterous, says Stone, that such an individual respects the Constitution.

The Constitution has conferred on Congress the exclusive authority to prescribe uniform rules governing naturalization. Congress has exercised that power by prescribing the conditions, in conformity to which aliens may obtain the privilege of citizenship. Under the laws and Constitution of the United States, no person is given any right to demand citi-

Harlan Fiske Stone, dissenting opinion, *United States v. Schneiderman*, 320 U.S. 118, June 21, 1943.

zenship, save upon compliance with those conditions. 'An alien who seeks political rights as a member of this nation can rightfully obtain them only upon terms and conditions specified by Congress. Courts are without authority to sanction changes or modifications; their duty is rigidly to enforce the legislative will in respect of a matter so vital to the public welfare.' And whenever a person's right to citizenship is drawn in question, it is judge's duty loyally to see to it that those conditions have not been disregarded.

The present suit by the United States, to cancel petitioner's previously granted certificate of citizenship, was brought pursuant to an Act of Congress, enacted long prior to petitioner's naturalization. Section 15 authorizes any court by a suit instituted by the United States Attorney to set aside a certificate of naturalization 'on the ground of fraud or on the ground that such certificate of citizenship was illegally procured'. Until now this Court, without a dissenting voice, has many times held that in a suit under this statute it is the duty of the court to render a judgment cancelling the certificate of naturalization if the court finds upon evidence that the applicant did not satisfy the conditions which Congress had made prerequisite to the award of citizenship. . . .

Lack of Attachment to the Constitution's Principles Should Be Grounds for Cancellation

Section 15 authorizes and directs the Government to institute the suit to cancel the certificate of naturalization on the ground of fraud or on the ground that the certificate was illegally procured. Until now it has never been thought that a certificate of citizenship procured by one who has not satisfied statutory conditions for citizenship, is nevertheless lawfully procured. But the concurring opinion of Mr. Justice [William O.] Douglas suggests that, for purposes of 15, 'attachment to the principles of the Constitution' is not a condition of becoming a citizen. It suggests that the statute is satisfied, even though the applicant was never in fact attached to the principles of the Constitution, so long as such attachment was made to appear, from pro forma affidavits, to the satisfaction of the naturalization court. This is said to be the case regardless of whether in fact the affidavits, and the certificate of citizenship based on them, are wholly mistaken. . . .

It would seem passing strange that Congress—which authorized cancellation of citizenship under 15 for failure to hold the naturalization hearing in open court instead of in the judge's chambers, or for failure to present the requisite certificate of arrival in this country—should be thought less concerned with the applicant's attachment to the principles of the Constitution and that he be well disposed to the good order and happiness of the United States. For what could be more important in the selection of citizens of the United States than that the prospective citizen be attached to the principles of the Constitution? . . .

Petitioner, who is an educated and intelligent man, took out his first papers in 1924, when he was eighteen years of age, and was admitted to citizenship on June 10, 1927, when nearly twenty-two. Since his sixteenth year he has been continuously and actively engaged in promoting in one way or another the interests of various Communist Party organizations affiliated with and controlled as to their policy and action by the Third International, the parent Communist organization, which had its headquarters and its Executive Committee in Moscow. The evidence shows petitioner's loyalty to the Communist Party organizations; that as a member of the Party he was subject to and accepted its political control, and that as a Party member his adherence to its political principles and tactics was required by its constitution.

The evidence shows and it is not denied that the Communist Party organization at the time in question was a revolutionary party having as its ultimate aim generally, and particularly in England and the United States, the overthrow of capitalistic government, and the substitution for it of the dictatorship of the proletariat. It sought to accomplish this through persistent indoctrination of the people in capitalistic countries with Party principles, by the organization in those countries of sections of the Third International, by systematic teaching of Party principles at meetings and classes held under Party auspices, and by the publication and distribution of Communist literature which constituted one of the basic principles of Party action.

In accordance with the policy established at its Second World Congress in 1920, the Party press was brought under Party control through ownership of the various publication agencies. Strict adherence to Party principles was demanded of all publications, which were required to be edited by Party members of proved loyalty to the proletarian revolution. Propaganda was required to conform to the program and decisions of the Third International. Editors were removed and Party members expelled for non-compliance. Publications not conforming to Party principles were barred from Party classes.

Many such Communist Party publications were introduced at the trial and constitute a large part of the evidence in this case. Perusal of the record can leave no doubt of petitioner's unqualified loyalty to the Communist Party. His continuous services to the Party for twenty years in a great variety of capacities, and his familiarity with Party programs and literature, are convincing proof of his complete devotion to Communist Party principles, and his desire to advance them. Throughout he has been a diligent student of Party publications. Many of them were used in the Communist classes of which he was educational director in the years immediately preceding his naturalization. All were particularly brought to his attention as they were introduced in evidence and excerpts relative to the issues were discussed in open court. Except as may be later noted, he did not deny familiarity with them or disavow their teachings. They were the official exposition of the doctrines of the Party to which he had formally pledged his allegiance, diligently disseminated by him for the indoctrination of his fellow countrymen, especially the members of the Youth organizations of the Party. In the circumstances, and especially in the absence of any disavowal by petitioner or the assertion by him of ignorance of the principles which they proclaimed, they are persuasive evidence of the nature and extent of his want of attachment to the principles of the Constitution. . . .

Communism Is Not Compatible with the Constitution

It would be little short of preposterous to assert that vigorous aid knowingly given by a pledged Party member in disseminating the Party teachings, to which reference has been made, is compatible with attachment to the principles of the Constitution. On the record before us it would be difficult for a trial judge to conclude that petitioner was not well aware that he was a member of and aiding a party which taught and advocated the overthrow of the Government of the United States by force and violence. It would be difficult also to find as a fact that petitioner behaved as a man attached to the principles of the Constitution. The trial judge found that he did not. And the same evidence would seem to furnish plain enough support for the trial judge's further finding that petitioner did not behave as a man attached 'to the good order and happiness' of the United States.

Petitioner's pledge of adherence to Communist Party principles and tactics, and his membership in the Communist organizations, were neither passive nor indolent. His testimony shows clearly that during the crucial years he was a young man of vigorous intellect and strong convictions. He spent his time actively arranging for the dissemination of a gospel of which he never has asserted either ignorance or disbelief. His wide acquaintance with Party literature, and his zealous promotion of Party interests for many years, preclude the supposition that he did not know the character of its teachings and did not aid in their advocacy. They are persuasive that he was without attachment to the constitutional principles which those teachings aimed to destroy. Yet the Court's opinion seems to tell us that the trier of fact must not examine petitioner's gospel to find out what kind of man he was, or even what his gospel was; that the trier of fact could not 'impute' to petitioner any genuine attachment to the doctrines of these organizations whose teachings he so assiduously spread. It might as well be said that it is impossible to infer that a man is attached to the principles of a religious movement from the fact that he conducts its prayer meetings, or, to take a more sinister example, that it could not be inferred that a man is a Nazi and consequently not attached to constitutional principles who, for more than five years, had diligently circulated the [Nazi] doctrines of *Mein Kampf.*

In neither case of course is the inference inevitable. It is possible, though not probable or normal, for one to be attached to principles diametrically opposed to those, to the dissemination of which he has given his life's best effort. But it is a normal and sensible inference which the trier of fact is free to make that his attachment is to those principles rather than to constitutional principles with which they are at war. A man can be known by the ideas he spreads as well as by the company he keeps. And when one does not challenge the proof that he has given his life to spreading a particular class of well-defined ideas, it is convincing evidence that his attachment is to them rather than their opposites. In this case it is convincing evidence that petitioner, at the time of his naturalization, was not entitled to the citizenship he procured because he was not attached to the principles of the Constitution of the United States and because he was not well disposed to the good order and happiness of the same.

"New attempts to augment the Executive Branch's powers are generating fresh points of controversy in the nation's debate over balancing national security and constitutionally guaranteed civil liberties."

The Schneiderman Case Is Newly Relevant in the Age of the War on Terror

Charles H. Hooker

As the Schneiderman *case came about during a time of tension leading up to World War II, it is fitting the case would be revived as a major turning point in civil rights during the War on Terror. Just as federal officials were worried about William Schneiderman's loyalty to the United States because he professed a belief in communism, today security officials question the loyalty of some fundamentalist Muslims.* Schneiderman *provides a strong protection for Muslims and others today who might be caught up in investigations into terrorism. As Charles H. Hooker shows, the decision in* Schneiderman *has been reinforced over the years; the government must meet a strong burden of proof to denaturalize a naturalized citizen. Hooker is the former editor-in-chief of the* Emory International Law Review.

Imagine the following. From somewhere in middle-America, compelled by an advertisement while surfing the web, you send money to an international environmental charity, "Sea

Charles H. Hooker, "The Past as Prologue: *Schneiderman v. United States* and Contemporary Questions of Citizenship and Denationalization," *Emory International Law Review*, vol. 19, 2005, pp. 35–90. Copyright © 2005 Emory University School of Law. Reproduced by permission of publisher and author.

Peace," to save your favorite species of endangered marine life. As a U.S. citizen, you believe you are merely exercising basic First Amendment rights. The following month, Sea Peace activists peacefully obstruct a U.S. registered research vessel in the Indian Ocean to protest the research company's disregard for the nearly extinct species that captured your conscientious concern. In the confrontation that follows, a research vessel crew member falls overboard and drowns. Under the broad, new definition of "terrorism" enacted under the Patriot Act and other subsequently proposed legislation, the government charges the Sea Peace protestors with terrorism. If extradited to the United States, they may face the death penalty. As their patron, you may be precariously positioned as well. When prosecutors subpoena a list of Sea Peace donors, you could be indicted for "material support" of terrorism, and face time in prison with the possibilty of losing your citizenship.

Schneiderman and The War on Terror

As the "War on Terror" evolves, now four years after the events of September 11, 2001, journalists, legal scholars, and civil rights groups have formulated such scenarios in reaction to various pieces of legislation recently proposed by its chief proponents. The government's initial reactions to September 11th, such as the Patriot Act and the creation of the Department of Homeland Security through the Homeland Security Act of 2002, have been amply detailed, debated, and discussed. However, new attempts to augment the Executive Branch's powers are generating fresh points of controversy in the nation's debate over balancing national security and constitutionally guaranteed civil liberties.

One recent controversy focuses on citizenship and the possibility of stripping it from persons who support, or become members of, organizations deemed terrorist groups by the Executive Branch. As proponents of the War on Terror attempt to enact such denationalization measures, civil liberties advocates respond with counterproposals to block, mollify, or obliterate their effect. Journalists, activists, and presidential candidates have joined the fray with their own opinions, polemics, and propositions. This Comment [article] views the recent controversy over denationalization legislation as an occasion to resurrect the largely forgotten, yet seminal 1943 case of *Schneiderman v. United States*, in which the Supreme Court blocked a government attempt to strip citizenship from a naturalized immigrant citizen due to his affiliation with the Communist Party. In so ruling, the Court established a higher burden of proof for denaturalization proceedings and launched a line of case law with broad ramifications in denationalization law that speaks to questions raised by current legislation and debate. . . .

Denationalization Law After *Schneiderman*

Denationalization is a concept of international law that encompasses both denaturalization and expatriation. Denaturalization refers to the process of abrogating a citizen's naturalization on grounds of invalidity, material misrepresentation, illegal procurement, or non-attachment to constitutional principles at the time of naturalization. Most often, denaturalization attacks are lodged as procedural defects in the naturalization itself. For instance, a person may be denaturalized for having misrepresented a material fact during the naturalization process, such as his or her criminal record or duration of residency in the United States.

Expatriation consists of actions to divest citizenship from a citizen, whether natural born or naturalized, when the citizen is judged to have voluntarily and intentionally relinquished his or her citizenship through certain specified expatriative acts, such as declaring allegiance to another country, formally renouncing U.S. citizenship, or fighting for a foreign army engaged in hostilities against the United States. The following analysis traces the impact of *Schneiderman*, first through denaturalization cases and then through decisions in the realm of expatriation.

A Follow Up Case

Schneiderman had an immediate impact on denaturalization proceedings. The most immediate reverberations appeared one year later when the Court again took the opportunity to assert a stringent standard for stripping citizenship in *Baumgartner v. United States*. Carl Wilhelm Baumgartner immigrated to the United States from Germany in 1927. He soon began working at Kansas City Power and Light Company, and in 1932 the U.S. District Court for the Western District of Missouri admitted Baumgartner to U.S. citizenship. A decade later, the United States brought suit against Baumgartner, claiming, as in *Schneiderman*, that he illegally and fraudulently procured his citizenship. Whereas in *Schneiderman* the government argued that Schneiderman "had not behaved as, a person attached to the principles of the Constitution of the United States," the government in this case contended that Baumgartner "did not truly and fully renounce his allegiance to Germany and that he did not in fact intend to support the Constitution and laws of the United States and to give them true faith and allegiance."

To support its allegations, the government presented a litany of damning evidence. Baumgartner's work supervisor testified that Baumgartner "spoke so persistently about the superiority of German people, the German schools, and the engineering work of Germans, that he aroused antagonism among his co-workers and was transferred to a different section of the plant." Discontented with the Weimer Republic, then in control of Germany, Baumgartner extolled the virtues of [Adolf] Hitler and Nazism, both at work and in the surrounding community. He made at least three public speeches commending the accomplishments of the Nazi government and indicating "he would be glad to live under the regime of Hitler." In the late 1930s, when German invasions commenced, Baumgartner commented, "Today I am rejoicing." Baumgartner's diary revealed his "violent anti-Semitism, impatience at the lack of pro-German militancy [among] German-Americans, and approval of Germans who have not 'been Americanized, that is, ruined.'" When the trial judge asked him, "[W]as your attitude towards the principles of the American government in 1932 when you took the oath the same as it has been ever since," he responded affirmatively. The district court entered a decree for the government. The Eighth Circuit affirmed.

Full Equality for Naturalized Citizens

The Supreme Court, however, reversed. While a five to three majority announced the "clear, unequivocal, and convincing" burden of proof for revoking citizenship in *Schneiderman*, a unanimous Court now embraced this more stringent evidentiary standard. After dissenting in *Schneiderman*, Justice [Felix] Frankfurter wrote for the majority in *Baumgartner*. Frankfurter's opinion insisted on a stringent evidentiary standard despite [section] 338 of the Nationality Act of 1940, which articulated less rigorous requirements for revoking citizenship. Significantly, Frankfurter and the Court grounded their insistence on an exacting standard for revoking citizenship in the Constitution. While Article I, [section] 8, clause 4 of the Constitution empowers Congress to erect statutory requirements for admission into citizenship, once nationalized, "a naturalized citizen stands on an equal footing with the native citizen in all respects, save that of eligibility to the Presidency." The Court continued:

> New relations and new interests flow, once citizenship has been granted. All that should not be undone unless the proof is compelling that that which was granted was obtained in defiance of Congressional authority. Non-

fulfillment of specific conditions, like time of residence or the required number of supporting witnesses, are easily established, and when established leave no room for discretion because Congress has left no area of discretion. But where the claim of "illegality" really involves issues of belief or fraud, proof is treacherous and objective judgment, even by the most disciplined minds, precarious. That is why denaturalization on this score calls for weighty proof.

Aware and "fully mindful that due observance of the law governing the grant of citizenship to aliens touches the very well-being of the Nation," the Court nevertheless adamantly insisted that "citizenship once bestowed should not be in jeopardy nor in fear of exercising its American freedom through a too easy finding that citizenship was disloyally acquired."

Denaturalization Requires Clear Proof of Disloyalty

Justice [Frank] Murphy's concurrence made the point more strongly, stating that "American citizenship is not a right granted on a condition subsequent that the naturalized citizen refrain in the future from uttering any remark or adopting an attitude favorable to his original homeland or those there in power, no matter how distasteful such conduct may be to most of us." The government's "clear, unequivocal, and convincing" burden of proof "transcends the particular ground upon which the Government seeks to set aside [a] naturalization certificate . . . [and] is equally applicable whether the citizen against whom the proceeding is brought is a Communist, a Nazi or a follower of any other political faith."

Although Justice Frankfurter opined "[i]t is idle to try to capture and confine the spirit of this requirement of proof within any fixed form of words," subsequent decisions show that the *Baumgartner* Court cemented the "clear, unequivocal, and convincing" burden of proof as the evidentiary standard for denaturalization proceedings. Some courts have further interpreted Justice Frankfurter's words to hold that appellate review in denaturalization cases is broader in its power to review findings of fact in connection with this evidentiary standard. On the whole, the grave consequences for the individual citizen in combination with the dubious means by which disloyalty and fraud are established—in this case, through later recollections filtered by "the distorting and self-deluding medium of memory" of the time when citizenship was claimed—compelled the *Baumgartner* Court to affirm and even bolster the evidentiary test articulated by Justice Murphy in *Schneiderman*.

"The United States attempted to revoke Schneiderman's citizenship most likely to strike a blow against possible disloyalty."

The Issues of Loyalty Dealt with in the *Schneiderman* Case Are Relevant to Post-9/11 America

David Fontana

The arguments in the Schneiderman *case hinged on whether naturalized citizens advocating radical change in the American system of government can be trusted as being "attached to the constitutional principles of the United States." Schneiderman's lawyer, the Republican politician and defeated presidential candidate Wendell Willkie, argued that the Constitution itself was open to radical change. Article V, the section of the Constitution concerned with amending the document, forbid changes only in the matter of slavery (which was protected from being outlawed until 1808) and equal representation of the various states in the Senate. The founders imposed no other conditions on possible amendments. Therefore, a citizen—even a naturalized citizen— could advocate any sort of change and still be loyal to the Constitution. Chief Justice Harlan Fiske Stone dissented, holding that the principles advocated by the Communist Party were completely in disagreement with American conceptions of liberty and democracy. The majority, however, agreed that any sort of political speech was protected by the Constitution and that natu-*

David Fontana, "A Case for the Twenty-first Century Constitutional Canon: *Schneiderman v. United States*," *Connecticut Law Review*, vol. 35, 2002, pp. 35, 42–48. Copyright © 2002 Connecticut Law Review. Reproduced by permission.

ralized citizens could not be deported for advocating unpopular political ideas. The author of this article, David Fontana, is a professor at the George Washington University Law School.

Hidden in the basements of American law libraries and in the Westlaw and Lexis databases is a genially ignored 1943 case, *Schneiderman v. United States*. *Schneiderman* is a case of substantial importance, and interest that has belonged in the constitutional canon for some time. In *Schneiderman*, the Supreme Court of the United States blocked the government's attempt to denaturalize an American citizen, a leader of the Communist Party, because the Court found that Communists could be "attached to the principles of the Constitution." The Court also announced a new, relatively high evidentiary burden that the government has to meet in order to strip naturalized citizens of their citizenship.

Schneiderman is of even greater importance after September 11, 2001, because it sheds light on several key issues facing both this country and its law students and lawyers. . . .

Terms of Naturalization

William Schneiderman became a citizen of the United States in 1927. Schneiderman was naturalized in 1927, although he was an active member of the Workers (Communist) Party of America and the Young Workers (Communist) League of America. The statute governing naturalizations at the time stated:

> It shall be made to appear to the satisfaction of the court admitting any alien to citizenship that immediately preceding the date of his application he has resided continuously within the United States five years at least, and within the State or Territory where such court is at the time held one year at least, and that during that time he has behaved as a man of good moral character, *attached to the principles of the Constitution of the United States*, and well disposed to

the good order and happiness of the same. In addition to the oath of the applicant, the testimony of at least two witnesses, citizens of the United States, as to the facts of residence, moral character, and attachment to the principles of the Constitution shall be required, and the name, place of residence, and occupation of each witness shall be set forth in the record.

Thus, in order to be naturalized as a citizen, Schneiderman had to claim to be a person "attach[ed] to the principles of the Constitution" of the United States. Schneiderman did precisely that, and he became a naturalized citizen of the United States.

A Test Case

In the late 1930s and early 1940s, with the war in Europe just beginning, political pressure obviously encouraged governmental leaders to persecute and even prosecute allegedly disloyal citizens. At the same time, American attention began to focus more on the danger posed by the Communist Soviet Union. Therefore, in 1939, the United States attempted to revoke Schneiderman's citizenship most likely to strike a blow against possible disloyalty, especially pro-Communist or pro-Nazi behavior at a time when the Soviet Union was fighting against American interests in World War II.

The United States relied on Section 15 of the 1906 statute, which authorized the United States Attorney General to institute a suit to set aside a certificate of naturalization "on the ground of fraud or on the ground that such certificate of citizenship was illegally procured." The United States relied upon the second of these grounds (illegally procured citizenship) in its denaturalization lawsuit because it asserted that Schneiderman's communist activity meant that he could not be "attached to the principles of the Constitution of the United States." The federal district court in California ruled in favor of the government and revoked Schneiderman's citizenship, finding that Schneiderman had pursued "unconstitutional objectives by unconstitutional means." The Ninth Circuit Court of Appeals affirmed the lower court's decision, stating that:

> There was substantial evidence which, if believed, leads to the conclusion that the Communist Party held and advocated that private ownership of the agents of production was wrong; that the agents of production should be confiscated by the government without compensation to the private owners thereof, that the government should be a dictatorship of the proletariat; that the present government here should be abandoned and one like that of the Soviet Union established; that the Supreme Court and the Senate should he abolished; that the government should be controlled by one political party only, and all others should be suppressed; and that the various countries of the world should establish a world union of Soviet Socialist Republics. *It is obvious that these views are not those of our Constitution.*

The Government Case

Schneiderman appealed to the United States Supreme Court. The case attracted a lot of attention and a number of prominent lawyers, even for a Supreme Court case. Solicitor General Charles Fahy argued for the government, focusing on the meaning of the statutory language "attach[ed] to the principles of the Constitution" of the United States. Fahy argued that holding a belief "that the laws and the Constitution should be amended in some or many respects" was not enough to prove non-attachment to the Constitution. An alien must, according to Fahy, "belie[ve] in and sincere[ly] adhere to" the Constitution's "general political philosophy." Fahy presented a test to see if an alien was attached to the general political philosophy of the Constitution:

> The test is . . . whether [an alien] substitutes revolution for evolution, destruction for construction, whether he believes in an ordered society, a government of laws, under which the powers of government are granted by the people but

under a grant which itself preserves to the individual and to minorities certain rights or freedoms which even the majority may not take away; whether, in sum, the events which began at least no further back than the Declaration of Independence, followed by the Revolutionary War and the adoption of the Constitution, establish principles with respect to government, the individual, the minority and the majority, by which ordered liberty is replaced by disorganized liberty.

Thus, according to Fahy, there is a hierarchy of principles within the Constitution, with some principles more fundamental than others. To believe in the Constitution means believing in these fundamental principles, and to believe in the Constitution means that you cannot believe in changing these principles.

A Decision for Free Speech

Arguing for Schneiderman, the recently defeated 1940 Republican presidential candidate Wendell Willkie asserted that the absence of substantive limitations on changes in Article V, beyond the slavery and equal representation provisos, meant that "a person can be attached to the Constitution no matter how extensive the changes are that he desires, so long as he seeks to achieve his ends within the framework of Article V." . . .

The Court agreed with Willkie, although it stopped short of adopting an obviously temporary proceduralist interpretation of the Constitution. Justice Frank Murphy wrote the opinion of the Court, emphasizing a constitutional procedural point: For constitutional reasons, the government cannot set aside an award of citizenship "years after it was granted."

Because of the grave loss suffered by a denaturalized citizen and the constitutional status of that loss, the Constitution requires that his citizenship could only be taken away with "the clearest sort of justification and proof." Justice Murphy discussed what it means to be "attached to the principles of the Constitution of the United States," using the First Amendment to dictate his interpretation of that phase. Justice Murphy looked at Communist documents that called for the abolition of private property without compensation, the establishment of a proletarian dictatorship with political rights denied to persons who were not proletarian and/or members of the Party, and the creation of an international union of Soviet Republics, and concluded that believing in these doctrines did not necessarily mean that one was not attached to the principles of the Constitution. Justice Murphy wrote that "[t]he constitutional fathers, fresh from a revolution, did not forge a political strait-jacket for the generations to come." Justice Murphy emphasized the presence of Article V, coupled with the "many important and far-reaching changes made in the Constitution since 1787," and argued that these changes "refute the idea that attachment to any particular provision or provisions is essential, or that one who advocates radical changes is necessarily not attached to the Constitution."

Divided Opinions

Justice William O. Douglas wrote a concurring opinion, arguing that the 1906 statute should be interpreted to mean that only fraud could be a basis for revoking naturalization. Justice Wiley Rutledge concurred, arguing that revoking Schneiderman's citizenship would result in a permanent two-class system of citizenship, whereby naturalized American citizens had to perpetually fear that they were in danger of being deported. Chief Justice Harlan Fiske Stone wrote the dissenting opinion (joined by Justices Felix Frankfurter and Owen Roberts) adopting Fahy's arguments. Chief Justice Stone believed that there was a hierarchy of principles in the Constitution, and that attachment to the Constitution means that one had to believe in certain fundamental constitutional principles, which he defined as, "[t]he principle of constitutional protection of civil rights and of life, liberty and property, the principle of representative government, and the principle that constitutional laws are not to be broken down by planned disobedience." Chief Justice Stone continued:

> I assume also that all the principles of the Constitution are hostile to dictatorship and minority rule; and that it is a principle of our Constitution that change in the organization of our government is to be effected by the orderly procedures ordained by the Constitution and not by force or fraud.

Chief Justice Stone examined Communist party documents ranging from [Joseph] Stalin's *Theory and Practice of Leninism* to the *ABCs of Communism*. The Chief Justice concluded from these and other documents that the Party—and therefore Schneiderman—was committed to violent revolution and overthrowing the fundamental principles of the United States Constitution. If Schneiderman had his way, according to Chief Justice Stone, then there would be an abandonment of "existing constitutional principles" and the basic core of the "freedoms guaranteed by the Bill of Rights [would] be ended." Therefore, Chief Justice Stone had no problem concluding that the record demonstrated "a basis for finding in the Party teachings, during the period in question, an unqualified hostility to the most fundamental and universally recognized principles of the Constitution."

Deportation Requires Clear and Compelling Evidence

The *Schneiderman* case is particularly fascinating for the range of discussions and rulings in the opinions of the Court. As partially compelled by the First Amendment and the general constitutional design, the majority interpreted the phrase "attached to the principles of the Constitution" to mean that the Constitution was a "limited absolute/hierarchical entrenchment" document. Also, as dictated by the Constitution's protection of fundamental liberties, the Court held that citizenship could not be stripped without the most clear and compelling evidence. The Court issued these rulings in 1943, a crucial year during World War II when domestic pressure to crack down on dissenters and critics of the American system was seemingly at its greatest.

CHAPTER 3

Debating Illegal Immigrant Children's Right to Public Education

Case Overview

Plyler v. Doe (1982)

In May 1975 the state legislature in Texas passed a law (section 21.031 of the Texas Education Code) allowing local school districts to deny free access to education to children illegally in the country. In September 1977, organizations representing these children, all from Mexico, filed suit in the U.S. District Court for East Texas in order to block the law and secure access to free public education. The case was ultimately decided by the Supreme Court under the name of *Plyler v. Doe*, in June 1982. The Court was strongly divided over the case, but the 5 to 4 majority went in favor of the illegal immigrant schoolchildren.

The majority ruling, issued by William Brennan, held that there was no rational basis for the state to discriminate against these children. Brennan based his decision on several points. First, they were for all intents and purposes permanent residents of the United States, with little likelihood they would return to Mexico. Denying them education would create a permanent class of uneducated inhabitants of Texas. Second, the federal government had shown no sign of trying to deport their parents, also illegal immigrants. They had tacit permission to remain in the country, and thus should be accorded the rights of legal residents. Third, the Texas law would not have much effect on the quality of education in the state as the number of children that would be denied access was relatively small. Finally, the Texas statute would not have any meaningful impact on deterring illegal immigration, thus there was no purpose in discriminating against these children on the basis of their immigration status.

The dissenters on the Court saw things differently. First, it was not the Court's job to second-guess public policy; Congress and the legislatures of the various states were allowed to make mistakes as long as they were not explicitly unconstitutional. While it may be foolish to deny education to a certain class of children, there was certainly a rational basis to deny a government benefit to persons with no legal right even to be in the country. Thus the Texas legislature was well within its constitutional rights in stopping illegal aliens from obtaining a publicly funded benefit. Finally, while the majority was of the opinion that the educational effect of preventing the enrollment of the children in schools would be minimal, that decision should be left to the political branches who were best in a position to make the judgment. It was certainly rational to believe that the savings derived in not allowing the children to attend school would go to benefit children legally in the country.

The *Plyler v. Doe* decision is still hotly debated. The concept of educational benefits for illegal immigrant children has gained political support in Congress and state legislatures, with some laws even allowing, under certain circumstances, university and college educational benefits for illegal immigrants. At the same time the general public is skeptical; in 1994 a measure was passed in California seeking to deny public benefits, including education, to illegal immigrants. It is possible, given the uproar over immigration, that such a law could be passed again today.

"By denying these children a basic education, we deny them the ability to live within the structure of our civic institutions."

The Court's Decision: States Cannot Bar Illegal Immigrant Children from Public Education

William J. Brennan

William J. Brennan, an influential liberal justice of the twentieth century, was appointed to the Supreme Court by President Dwight D. Eisenhower in 1956, and served until retiring in 1990. In this decision, Justice Brennan argues that illegal immigrant children are covered under the Fourteenth Amendment's provisions of "equal protection under the law" and by the due process clause of the same amendment. While public education is not a fundamental right, according to Brennan the denial of free basic education will deprive these children of the chance to advance in life and contribute to the national society. In addition, Brennan holds that Texas has shown no rational basis for denying education to illegal immigrant children: denying such education will not deter illegal immigration, and providing such education will not significantly affect on the quality of education for the other children in the state.

Sheer incapability or lax enforcement of the laws barring entry into this country, coupled with the failure to establish an effective bar to the employment of undocumented

William J. Brennan, majority opinion, *Plyler v. Doe*, June 15, 1982.

alien, has resulted in the creation of a substantial "shadow population" of illegal migrant—numbering in the millions— within our borders. This situation raises the specter of a permanent [457 U.S. 202, 219] caste of undocumented resident aliens, encouraged by some to remain here as a source of cheap labor, but nevertheless denied the benefits that our society makes available to citizens and lawful residents. The existence of such an underclass presents most difficult problems for a Nation that prides itself on adherence to principles of equality under law.

Children Deserve Special Protection

The children who are plaintiffs in these cases are special members of this underclass. Persuasive arguments support the view that a State may withhold its beneficence from those whose very presence within the United States is the product of their own unlawful conduct. These arguments do not apply with the same force to classifications imposing disabilities on the minor children of such illegal entrants. At the least, those who elect to enter our territory by stealth and in violation of our law should be prepared to bear the consequences, including, but not limited to, deportation. But the children of those illegal entrants are not comparably situated. Their "parents have the ability to conform their conduct to societal norms," and presumably the ability to remove themselves from the State's jurisdiction; but the children who are plaintiffs in these cases "can affect neither their parents' conduct nor their own status." Even if the State found it expedient to control the conduct of adults by acting against their children, legislation directing the onus of a parent's misconduct against his children does not comport with fundamental conceptions of justice.

> [V]isiting . . . condemnation on the head of an infant is illogical and unjust. Moreover, imposing disabilities on the . . . child is contrary to the basic concept of our system that legal burdens should bear some relationship to individual

responsibility or wrongdoing. Obviously, no child is responsible for his birth and penalizing the . . . child is an ineffectual—as well as unjust—way of deterring the parent.

Of course, undocumented status is not irrelevant to any proper legislative goal. Nor is undocumented status an absolutely immutable characteristic since it is the product of conscious, indeed unlawful, action. But 21.03 [the Texas law barring illegal alien children from public education] is directed against children, and imposes its discriminatory burden on the basis of a legal characteristic over which children can have little control. It is thus difficult to conceive of a rational justification for penalizing these children for their presence within the United States. Yet that appears to be precisely the effect of 21.031.

Public Education Is Uniquely Important

Public education is not a "right" granted to individuals by the Constitution. But neither is it merely some governmental "benefit" indistinguishable from other forms of social welfare legislation. Both the importance of education in maintaining our basic institutions, and the lasting impact of its deprivation on the life of the child, mark the distinction. The "American people have always regarded education and [the] acquisition of knowledge as matters of supreme importance." We have recognized "the public schools as a most vital civic institution for the preservation of a democratic system of government," and as the primary vehicle for transmitting "the values on which our society rests." "[A]s . . . pointed out early in our history, . . . some degree of education is necessary to prepare citizens to participate effectively and intelligently in our open political system if we are to preserve freedom and independence." And these historic "perceptions of the public schools as inculcating, fundamental values necessary to the maintenance of a democratic political system have been confirmed by the observations of social scientists." In addition, education provides the basic tools by which individuals might lead economically productive lives to the benefit of us all. In sum, education has a fundamental role in maintaining the fabric of our society. We cannot ignore the significant social costs borne by our Nation when select groups are denied the means to absorb the values and skills upon which our social order rests.

In addition to the pivotal role of education in sustaining our political and cultural heritage, denial of education to some isolated group of children poses an affront to one of the goals of the Equal Protection Clause: the abolition of governmental barriers presenting unreasonable obstacles to advancement on the basis of individual merit. Paradoxically, by depriving the children of any disfavored group of an education, we foreclose the means by which that group might raise the level of esteem in which it is held by the majority. But more directly, "education prepares individuals to be self-reliant and self-sufficient participants in society." Illiteracy is an enduring disability. The inability to read and write will handicap the individual deprived of a basic education each and every day of his life. The inestimable toll of that deprivation on the social, economic, intellectual, and psychological well-being of the individual, and the obstacle it poses to individual achievement, make it most difficult to reconcile the cost or the principle of a status-based denial of basic education with the framework of equality embodied in the Equal Protection Clause. What we said 28 years ago in *Brown v. Board of Education*, [the decison outlawing segregated schools] still holds true:

> Today, education is perhaps the most important function of state and local governments. Compulsory school attendance laws and the great expenditures for education both demonstrate our recognition of the importance of education to our democratic society. It is required in the performance of our most basic public responsibilities, even service in the armed forces. It is the very foundation of good citizenship. Today it is a principal instrument in awakening the child to cultural

values, in preparing him for later professional training, and in helping him to adjust normally to his environment. In these days, it is doubtful that any child may reasonably be expected to succeed in life if he is denied the opportunity of an education. Such an opportunity, where the state has undertaken to provide it, is a right which must be made available to all on equal terms.

The Texas Law Imposes a Lifetime of Hardship

These well-settled principles allow us to determine the proper level of deference to be afforded 21.031. Undocumented aliens cannot be treated as a suspect class because their presence in this country in violation of federal law is not a "constitutional irrelevancy." Nor is education a fundamental right; a State need not justify by compelling necessity every variation in the manner in which education is provided to its population. But more is involved in these cases than the abstract question whether 21.031 discriminates against a suspect class, or whether education is a fundamental right. Section 21.031 imposes a lifetime hardship on a discrete class of children not accountable for their disabling status. The stigma of illiteracy will mark them for the rest of their lives. By denying these children a basic education, we deny them the ability to live within the structure of our civic institutions, and foreclose any realistic possibility that they will contribute in even the smallest way to the progress of our Nation. In determining the rationality of 21.031, we may appropriately take into account its costs to the Nation and to the innocent children who are its victims. In light of these countervailing costs, the discrimination, contained in 21.031 can hardly be considered rational unless it furthers some substantial goal of the State.

It is the State's principal argument, and apparently the view of the dissenting Justices, that the undocumented status of these children *vel non* [or Their legal status] establishes a sufficient rational basis for denying them benefits that a State might choose to afford other residents. The State notes that while other aliens are admitted "on an equality of legal privileges with all citizens under non-discriminatory laws," the asserted right of these children to an education can claim no implicit congressional imprimatur. Indeed, in the State's view, Congress' apparent disapproval of the presence of these children within the United States, and the evasion of the federal regulatory program that is the mark of undocumented status, provides authority for its decision to impose upon them special disabilities. Faced with an equal protection challenge respecting the treatment of aliens, we agree that the courts must be attentive to congressional policy; the exercise of congressional power might well affect the State's prerogatives to afford differential treatment to a particular class of aliens. But we are unable to find in the congressional immigration scheme any statement of policy that might weigh significantly in arriving at an equal protection balance concerning the State's authority to deprive these children of an education. . . .

Denying Children Education is Not an Effective Deterrent to Illegal Immigration

Appellants [The State of Texas] argue that the classification at issue furthers an interest in the "preservation of the state's limited resources for the education of its lawful residents." Of course, a concern for the preservation of resources standing alone can hardly justify the classification used in allocating those resources. The State must do more than justify its classification with a concise expression of an intention to discriminate. Apart from the asserted state prerogative to act against undocumented children solely on the basis of their undocumented status—an asserted prerogative that carries only minimal force in the circumstances of these cases—we discern three colorable state interests that might support 21.031.

First, appellants appear to suggest that the State may seek to protect itself from an influx of illegal immigrants. While a

State might have an interest in mitigating the potentially harsh economic effects of sudden shifts in population, 21.031 hardly offers an effective method of dealing with an urgent demographic or economic problem. There is no evidence in the record suggesting that illegal entrants impose any significant burden on the State's economy. To the contrary, the available evidence suggests that illegal aliens underutilize public services, while contributing their labor to the local economy and tax money to the state fisc. The dominant incentive for illegal entry into the State of Texas is the availability of employment; few if any illegal immigrants come to this country, or presumably to the State of Texas, in order to avail themselves of a free education. Thus, even making the doubtful assumption that the net impact of illegal aliens on the economy of the State is negative, we think it clear that "[c]harging tuition to undocumented children constitutes a ludicrously ineffectual attempt to stem the tide of illegal immigration," at least when compared with the alternative of prohibiting the employment of illegal aliens.

Illegal Alien Children Do Not Hurt the Quality of Education

Second, while it is apparent that a State may "not . . . reduce expenditures for education by barring [some arbitrarily chosen class of] children from its schools," appellants suggest that undocumented children are appropriately singled out for exclusion because of the special burdens they impose on the State's ability to provide high-quality public education. But the record in no way supports the claim that exclusion of undocumented children is likely to improve the overall quality of education in the State . . . the State failed to offer any "credible supporting evidence that a proportionately small diminution of the funds spent on each child [which might result from devoting some state funds to the education of the excluded group] will have a grave impact on the quality of education."

And, after reviewing the State's school financing mechanism, the District Court ... concluded that barring undocumented children from local schools would not necessarily improve the quality of education provided in those schools. Of course, even if improvement in the quality of education were a likely result of barring some number of children from the schools of the State, the State must support its selection of this group as the appropriate target for exclusion. In terms of educational cost and need, however, undocumented children are "basically indistinguishable" from legally resident alien children.

Finally, appellants suggest that undocumented children are appropriately singled out because their unlawful presence within the United States renders them less likely than other children to remain within the boundaries of the State, and to put their education to productive social or political use within the State. Even assuming that such an interest is legitimate, it is an interest that is most difficult to quantify. The State has no assurance that any child, citizen or not, will employ the education provided by the State within the confines of the State's borders. In any event, the record is clear that many of the undocumented children disabled by this classification will remain in this country indefinitely, and that some will become lawful residents or citizens of the United States. It is difficult to understand precisely what the State hopes to achieve by promoting the creation and perpetuation of a subclass of illiterates within our boundaries, surely adding to the problems and costs of unemployment, welfare, and crime. It is thus clear that whatever savings might be achieved by denying these children an education, they are wholly insubstantial in light of the costs involved to these children, the State, and the Nation.

If the State is to deny a discrete group of innocent children the free public education that it offers to other children residing within its borders, that denial must be justified by a showing that it furthers some substantial state interest. No such showing was made here. Accordingly, the judgment of the Court of Appeals in each of these cases is affirmed.

> "It simply is not 'irrational' for a state
> to conclude that it does not have the
> ... responsibility to provide benefits for
> persons whose very presence in the state
> and this country is illegal."

Dissenting Opinion: Denying Free Education to Illegal Aliens Is Not Unconstitutional

Warren Burger

In this decision Chief Justice Warren Burger criticizes the majority in Plyler v. Doe *for interfering in educational policy, an area reserved for the state legislatures. While Burger personally believes that Texas law 21.031 (denying illegal alien children enrollment in public schools) is foolish policy, he rejects that it contradicts the Fourteenth Amendment's guarantee of equal protection. Burger notes that in a variety of areas, the Court has ruled that states can withhold benefits from those not resident in the state or not legally in the state. Remarking that it is not irrational to distinguish between lawful and illegal residents, Burger holds that education is simply another benefit that legislatures can deny to persons who are not legally in their state. Burger was chief justice of the Supreme Court from 1969 to 1986.*

Were it our business to set the Nation's social policy, I would agree without hesitation that it is senseless for an enlightened society to deprive any children—including illegal aliens—of an elementary education. I fully agree that it would be folly—and wrong—to tolerate creation of a segment

Warren Burger, dissenting opinion, *Plyler v. Doe*, June 15, 1982.

of society made up of illiterate persons, many having a limited or no command of our language. However, the Constitution does not constitute us as "Platonic Guardians" nor does it vest in this Court the authority to strike down laws because they do not meet our standards of desirable social policy, "wisdom," or "common sense." We trespass on the assigned function of the political branches under our structure of limited and separated powers when we assume a policymaking role as the Court does today.

The Court Abuses Its Power

The Court makes no attempt to disguise that it is acting to make up for Congress' lack of "effective leadership" in dealing with the serious national problems caused by the influx of uncountable millions of illegal aliens across our borders. The failure of enforcement of the immigration laws over more than a decade and the inherent difficulty and expense of sealing our vast borders have combined to create a grave socioeconomic dilemma. It is a dilemma that has not yet even been fully assessed, let alone addressed. However, it is not the function of the Judiciary to provide "effective leadership" simply because the political branches of government fail to do so.

The Court's holding today manifests the justly criticized judicial tendency to attempt speedy and wholesale formulation of "remedies" for the failures—or simply the laggard pace—of the political processes of our system of government. The Court employs, and in my view abuses, the Fourteenth Amendment in an effort to become an omnipotent and omniscient problem solver. That the motives for doing so are noble and compassionate does not alter the fact that the Court distorts our constitutional function to make amends for the defaults of others.

In a sense, the Court's opinion rests on such a unique confluence of theories and rationales that it will likely stand for little beyond the results in these particular cases. Yet the extent to which the Court departs from principled constitutional adjudication is nonetheless disturbing.

I have no quarrel with the conclusion that the Equal Protection Clause of the Fourteenth Amendment applies to aliens who, after their illegal entry into this country, are indeed physically "within the jurisdiction" of a state. However, as the Court concedes, this "only begins the inquiry." The Equal Protection Clause does not mandate identical treatment of different categories of persons.

The dispositive issue in these cases, simply put, is whether, for purposes of allocating its finite resources, a state has a legitimate reason to differentiate between persons who are lawfully within the state and those who are unlawfully there. The distinction the State of Texas has drawn—based not only upon its own legitimate interests but on classifications established by the Federal Government in its immigration laws and policies—is not unconstitutional.

Ignoring Law to Reach a Desired Result

The Court acknowledges that, except in those cases when state classifications disadvantage a "suspect class" or impinge upon a "fundamental right," the Equal Protection Clause permits a state "substantial latitude" in distinguishing between different groups of persons. Moreover, the Court expressly—and correctly—rejects any suggestion that illegal aliens are a suspect class or that education is a fundamental right. Yet by patching together bits and pieces of what might be termed quasi-suspect-class and quasi-fundamental-rights analysis, the Court spins out a theory custom-tailored to the facts of these cases.

In the end, we are told little more than that the level of scrutiny employed to strike down the Texas law applies only when illegal alien children are deprived of a public education. If ever a court was guilty of an unabashedly result-oriented approach, this case is a prime example.

The Court first suggests that these illegal alien children, although not a suspect class, are entitled to special solicitude under the Equal Protection Clause because they lack "control" over or "responsibility" for their unlawful entry into this country. Similarly, the Court appears to take the position that 21.031 is presumptively "irrational" because it has the effect of imposing "penalties" on "innocent" children. However, the Equal Protection Clause does not preclude legislators from classifying among persons on the basis of factors and characteristics over which individuals may be said to lack "control." Indeed, in some circumstances persons generally, and children in particular, may have little control over or responsibility for such things as their ill health, need for public assistance, or place of residence. Yet a state legislature is not barred from considering, for example, relevant differences between the mentally healthy and the mentally ill, or between the residents of different counties, simply because these may be factors unrelated to individual choice or to any "wrongdoing." The Equal Protection Clause protects against arbitrary and irrational classifications, and against invidious discrimination stemming from prejudice and hostility; it is not an all-encompassing "equalizer" designed to eradicate every distinction for which persons are not "responsible." . . .

Education Not a Fundamental Right

The second strand of the Court's analysis rests on the premise that, although public education is not a constitutionally guaranteed right, "neither is it merely some governmental 'benefit' indistinguishable from other forms of social welfare legislation." Whatever meaning or relevance this opaque observation might have in some other context, it simply has no bearing on the issues at hand. Indeed, it is never made clear what the Court's opinion means on this score.

The importance of education is beyond dispute. Yet we have held repeatedly that the importance of a governmental service does not elevate it to the status of a "fundamental right" for purposes of equal protection analysis. In San Antonio Independent School Dist. Justice [Lewis] Powell, speaking for the Court, expressly rejected the proposition that state laws dealing with public education are subject to special scrutiny under the Equal Protection Clause. Moreover, the Court points to no meaningful way to distinguish between education and other governmental benefits in this context. Is the Court suggesting that education is more "fundamental" than food, shelter, or medical care?

The Equal Protection Clause guarantees similar treatment of similarly situated persons, but it does not mandate a constitutional hierarchy of governmental services. [Justice Powell] speaking for the Court in San Antonio put it well in stating that to the extent this Court raises or lowers the degree of "judicial scrutiny" in equal protection cases according to a transient Court majority's view of the societal importance of the interest affected, we "assum[e] a legislative role and one for which the Court lacks both authority and competence." Yet that is precisely what the Court does today.

The central question in these cases, as in every equal protection case not involving truly fundamental rights "explicitly or implicitly guaranteed by the Constitution," is whether there is some legitimate basis for a legislative distinction between different classes of persons. The fact that the distinction is drawn in legislation affecting access to public education—as opposed to legislation allocating other important governmental benefits, such as public assistance, health care, or housing—cannot make a difference in the level of scrutiny applied.

A Rational State Purpose

Once it is conceded—as the Court does—that illegal aliens are not a suspect class, and that education is not a fundamental right, our inquiry should focus on and be limited to whether the legislative classification at issue bears a rational relationship to a legitimate state purpose.

The State contends primarily that 21.031 serves to prevent undue depletion of its limited revenues available for education, and to preserve the fiscal integrity of the State's school-financing system against an ever-increasing flood of illegal aliens—aliens over whose entry or continued presence it has no control. Of course such fiscal concerns alone could not justify discrimination against a suspect class or an arbitrary and irrational denial of benefits to a particular group of persons. Yet I assume no Member of this Court would argue that prudent conservation of finite state revenues is per se an illegitimate goal. Indeed, the numerous classifications this Court has sustained in social welfare legislation were invariably related to the limited amount of revenues available to spend on any given program or set of programs. The significant question here is whether the requirement of tuition from illegal aliens who attend the public schools—as well as from residents of other states, for example—is a rational and reasonable means of furthering the State's legitimate fiscal ends.

Without laboring what will undoubtedly seem obvious to many, it simply is not "irrational" for a state to conclude that it does not have the same responsibility to provide benefits for persons whose very presence in the state and this country is illegal as it does to provide for persons lawfully present. By definition, illegal aliens have no right whatever to be here, and the state may reasonably, and constitutionally elect not to provide them with governmental services at the expense of those who are lawfully in the state. In *De Canas v. Bica* we held that a State may protect its "fiscal interests and lawfully resident labor force from the deleterious effects on its economy resulting from the employment of illegal aliens." And only recently this Court made clear that a State has a legitimate interest in protecting and preserving the quality of its schools and "the right of its own bona fide residents to attend such institution on a preferential tuition basis." The Court has failed to offer even a plausible explanation why illegality of residence in this country is not a factor that may legitimately bear upon the bona fides of state residence and entitlement to the benefits of lawful residence.

Illegal Aliens Excluded from Other Benefits

It is significant that the Federal Government has seen fit to exclude illegal aliens from numerous social welfare programs, such as the food stamp program, and the old-age assistance, aid to families with dependent children, aid to the blind, aid to the permanently and totally disabled, and supplemental security income programs, the Medicare hospital insurance benefits program, and the Medicaid hospital insurance benefits for the aged and disabled program. Although these exclusions do not conclusively demonstrate the constitutionality of the State's use of the same classification for comparable purposes, at the very least they tend to support the rationality of excluding illegal alien residents of a state from such programs so as to preserve the state's finite revenues for the benefit of lawful residents.

The Court maintains—as if this were the issue—that "barring undocumented children from local schools would not necessarily improve the quality of education provided in those schools." However, the legitimacy of barring illegal aliens from programs such as Medicare or Medicaid does not depend on a showing that the barrier would "improve the quality" of medical care given to persons lawfully entitled to participate in such programs. Modern education, like medical care, is enormously expensive, and there can be no doubt that very large added costs will fall on the State or its local school districts as a result of the inclusion of illegal aliens in the tuition-free public schools. The State may, in its discretion, use any savings resulting from its tuition requirement to "improve the quality of education" in the public school system, or to enhance the funds available for other social programs, or to reduce the tax burden placed on its residents; each of these ends is "legitimate." The State need not show, as the Court implies, that the incremental cost of educating illegal aliens will send it into bankruptcy, or have a "'grave impact on the quality of education,'" that is not dispositive under a "rational basis" scrutiny. In the absence of a constitutional imperative to provide for the education of illegal aliens, the State may "rationally" choose to take advantage of whatever savings will accrue from limiting access to the tuition-free public schools to its own lawful residents, excluding even citizens of neighboring States.

Denying a free education to illegal alien children is not a choice I would make were I a legislator. Apart from compassionate considerations, the long-range costs of excluding any children from the public schools may well outweigh the costs of educating them. But that is not the issue; the fact that there are sound policy arguments against the Texas Legislature's choice does not render that choice an unconstitutional one.

Plyler Is a Watershed Decision for Individual Rights

Michael A. Olivas

Supreme Court decisions rarely make such an impact as the 1982 Plyler *case, argues legal scholar Michael A. Olivas. The case established an important limit on states' ability to make policy regarding immigration. Moreover, it established the principle that a person is a resident where he or she lives, regardless of legal status. Over the decades since the decision,* Plyler *has become accepted by politicians to the point such that legislation has been passed that would extend* Plyler's *principles to college education. Olivas is the William B. Bates Distinguished Chair of Law and director of the Institute of Higher Education Law & Governance at the University of Texas.*

It is hard to know how Supreme Court decisions will come to be regarded, but one thing is certain: none of them exists in a vacuum. Getting a case to federal or state court in the first place is a lightning strike, and very few make it all the way through the chute to the Supreme Court. Fewer still are genuinely memorable, even within the specialty area in which the case is situated. *Plyler v. Doe* always stood for its resolution of the immediate issue in dispute: whether the State of Texas could enact laws denying undocumented children free access to its own public schools. But it also dealt with a larger,

Michael A. Olivas, "*Plyler v. Doe*, the Education of Undocumented Children, and the Polity," *Immigration Stories*, ed. David A. Martin and Peter H. Schuck. Eagan. MN: Foundation Press, 2005. Copyright © 2006 Foundation Press. Reproduced by permission.

transcendent principle: how this society will treat its alien children. Thus, for the larger polity, *Plyler* has become an important case for key themes, such as fairness for children, how we guard our borders, how we constitute ourselves, and who gets to make these crucial decisions. To a large extent, *Plyler* may also be the apex of the Court's treatment of the undocumented, a concept that never truly existed until the 20th century. . . .

The Supreme Court's Ruling

In June, 1982, the Supreme Court gave the schoolchildren their win on all counts, by a 5-4 margin. Justice [William] Brennan, in his majority opinion striking down the statute, characterized the Texas argument for charging tuition as "nothing more than an assertion that illegal entry, without more, prevents a person from becoming a resident for purposes of enrolling his children in the public schools." He employed an equal protection analysis to find that a State could not enact a discriminatory classification "merely by defining a disfavored group as non-resident."

Justice Brennan dismissed the State's first argument that the classification or subclass of undocumented Mexican children was necessary to preserve the State's "limited resources for the education of its lawful residents." This line of argumentation had been rejected in an earlier case, *Graham v. Richardson*, where the court had held that the concern for preservation of Arizona's resources alone could not justify an alienage classification used in allocating welfare benefits. In addition, he relied on the findings of fact from the *Plyler* trial: although the exclusion of all undocumented children might eventually result in some small savings to the state, those savings would be uncertain (given that federal and state allocations depended primarily upon the number of children enrolled), and barring those children would "not necessarily improve the quality of education."

Immigration Is a Federal Concern

The State also argued that it had enacted the legislation in order to protect itself from an influx of undocumented aliens. The Court acknowledged the concern, but found that the statute was not tailored to address it: "Charging tuition to undocumented children constitutes a ludicrously ineffectual attempt to stem the tide of illegal immigration." The Court also noted that immigration and naturalization policy is within the exclusive powers of federal government.

Finally, the state maintained that it singled out undocumented children because their unlawful presence rendered them less likely to remain in the United States and therefore to be able to use the free public education they received in order to contribute to the social and political goals of the United States community. Brennan distinguished the subclass of undocumented aliens who had lived in the United States as a family and for all practical purposes, permanently, from the subclass of adult aliens who enter the country alone, temporarily, to earn money. For those who remained with the intent of making the United States their home, "[i]t is difficult to understand precisely what the State hopes to achieve by promoting the creation and perpetuation of a subclass of illiterates within our boundaries, surely adding to the problems and costs of unemployment, welfare, and crime."

Prior to *Plyler*, the Supreme Court had never taken up the question of whether undocumented aliens could seek Fourteenth Amendment equal protection. The Supreme Court had long held that aliens are "persons" for purposes of the Fourteenth Amendment, and that undocumented aliens are protected by the due process provisions of the Fifth Amendment. However, Texas argued that because undocumented children were not "within its jurisdiction," they were not entitled to equal protection. Justice Brennan rejected this line of reasoning, concluding that there "is simply no support for [the] suggestion that 'due process' is somehow of greater stature than 'equal protection' and therefore available to a larger class of persons.". . .

A Watershed Decision

Much of the considerable scholarly response to the Court's reasoning in the case has evinced surprise that the majority went as far as it did in rejecting the state's sovereignty. Peter Schuck, for example, characterized the decision as a "conceptual watershed in immigration law, the most powerful rejection to date of classical immigration law's notion of plenary national sovereignty over our borders. . . . Courts are expositors of a constitutional tradition that increasingly emphasizes not the parochial and the situational, but the universal, transcendent values of equality and fairness immanent in the due process and equal protection principles. In that capacity, they have also asserted a larger role in the creation and distribution of opportunities and status in the administrative state. In *Plyler*, the Supreme Court moved boldly on both fronts." Surveying the line of equal protection cases involving aliens . . . [legal scholar] Linda Bosniak has summarized: "alienage as a legal status category means that the law of alienage discrimination is perennially burdened by the following questions: To what extent is such discrimination a legitimate expression, or extension, of the government's power to regulate the border and to control the composition of membership in the national community? On the other hand, how far does sovereignty reach before it must give way to equality; when, that is, does discrimination against aliens implicate a different kind of government power, subject to far more rigorous constraints? To what degree, in short, is the status of aliens to be understood as a matter of national borders, to what degree a matter of personhood, and how are we to tell the difference? These questions, I argue, shape the law's conflicted understandings of the difference that alienage makes."

Although *Plyler*'s incontestably bold reasoning has not substantially influenced subsequent Supreme Court immigration jurisprudence in the twenty-plus years since it was decided, the educational significance of the case is still clear, even if it is limited to this small subset of schoolchildren—largely Latinos—in the United States. Given the poor overall educational achievement evident in this population, even this one success story has significance. Again, the parallel to *Brown* [*v. Board of Education*, which ended school segregation] is striking: *Brown*'s legacy is questioned even after fifty years, largely due to Anglo racial intransigence and the failure of integration's promise.

Election Politics

In 1994, an unpopular governor of California, Pete Wilson, revived his reelection campaign by backing a ballot initiative known as Proposition 187, which would have denied virtually all state-funded benefits, including public education, to undocumented aliens. Proposition 187 passed with nearly 60 percent of the vote and Wilson was re-elected, but the federal courts enjoined implementation of most of the ballot measure, relying prominently on *Plyler*. During the congressional debates that eventually led to the enactment of the Illegal Immigration and Immigrant Responsibility Act of 1996, Representative Elton Gallegly (R.-Cal.) proposed an amendment that would have allowed states to charge tuition to undocumented students or exclude them from public schools. He was banking that, in the wake of such federal legislation, the courts would distinguish *Plyler* and sustain the state measure. The provision became quite politicized, receiving prominent support from Republican presidential candidate Robert Dole. Gallegly might have been right that the Constitution would not be read by the Court of the 1990s to nullify a federal enactment of the kind he proposed, but he never got a chance to find out, because *Plyler* proved to have considerable strength in the political arena. The Gallegly amendment drew heated opposition in Congress and in the media, and critics relied heavily on the values and arguments highlighted in *Plyler*—and often on the decision itself. After months of contentious debate, the amendment was dropped from the final legislation, and no provisions became law that restricted alien children's right to attend school. *Plyler* and the polity appear to have settled the question.

Although *Plyler* had addressed the issue of public school children in the K–12 setting, questions arose almost immediately after the ruling about how far the decision could be extended, notably whether it would protect undocumented college students. Before long, Peter Roos was going for the long ball again, litigating postsecondary *Plyler* cases in California. The cases have mostly denied relief, although the record is mixed. That history is for a companion volume, but I will say this: the ultimate irony is that in 2001, just after Governor George [W.] Bush left Texas to become President George Bush, the State enacted H.B. 1403, establishing the right of undocumented college students to establish resident status and pay in-state tuition in the State's public colleges. In the 25 years since Texas had enacted 21.031, this was silent testimony to the idea that you reside where you live, quite apart from your immigration status. A dozen states have acted since the Texas innovation. And in Congress, conservative Utah Senator Orrin Hatch co-authored the Development, Relief, and Education for Alien Minors (DREAM) Act. If enacted, it would remove a provision from federal law that discourages states from providing in-state tuition status to undocumented college students, and would also allow the students the opportunity to regularize their federal immigration status—an enormous benefit that would go well beyond what a state could provide. *Plyler* clearly is alive and well in its adolescence.

> "The Supreme Court held that these
> children were effectively discriminated
> against based on their national origin."

Plyler v. Doe Was a Blow to Racial Prejudice

Alejandra Rincón

Alejandra Rincón argues that the Plyler *decision protected Mexican illegal immigrant children from racial discrimination. Proponents of the law barring the undocumented from free public education argued in terms of educational quality and costs. The Supreme Court, however, saw that the proposed law would have little effect on education, other than to create a permanent underclass of the uneducated undocumented immigrants. The Court was also wary of past discrimination against Mexicans and Mexican Americans, and saw in the* Plyler *case a chance to ensure that history was not repeated. Rincón has served as the director of Multicultural Affairs at Prairie View A&M University and also as the adviser of Jovenes Inmigrantes por Futuro Mejor (Immigrant Youth for a Better Future), an association of immigrant college students throughout Texas.*

The focus of this paper is the Texas law that attempted to deny access to public education to the undocumented school age population and the ensuing Supreme Court decision, which reversed that policy. The students targeted by the

Alejandra Rincón, "The Intersection of Race and Ethnicity in *Plyler v. Doe*: Undocumented Children's Access to Public Education in Texas," *Topics in Education: Review of Research and Practice*, vol. 1, no. 1, 2004, pp. 1–6. Reproduced by permission.

Texas law are considered an ethnic group given their common Mexican ancestry and the fact that within the United States they are regarded as a minority based on their unequal treatment.

A critical race theory analysis inquires into the forms of racial prejudice, discrimination and institutional racism that exist in this society and the reality that immigration law and politics [according to R.J. Garcia] "have been historically intertwined with racial prejudice." From this perspective, the actions carried out by the State of Texas, the Texas Legislature, the Texas Educational Agency and the school districts had a differential and harmful impact on the members of this ethnicity, as the Supreme Court held that these children were effectively discriminated against based on their national origin. . . .

Historical Background

Since the 1840s, restrictive immigration policies have been periodically implemented to target immigrants as a form of manipulating labor markets, and in response to economic crisis, as well as political and social upsurges. While European arrivals were initially the target of xenophobia [fear of anything foreign] they were eventually able to assimilate. However, immigrants from the Third World have remained the target of harsh immigration policies, which have been able to brand them as an untouchable-like caste predicated upon easy identification largely based on skin color.

In the case of Mexico, immigration dates back to the signing of the Treaty of Guadalupe Hidalgo in 1848, when Mexico was forced to cede around half of its territory to the United States. Since then, there has been a long history of policies, which have attempted to either restrict or encourage the presence of Mexicans in the United States based on the requirements of U.S. business for a source of cheap labor (e.g. Bracero Program, Operation Wetback).

The governmental policies that have attempted to regulate the immigration patterns of Mexicans into the U.S. have gone hand in hand with similar restrictions to regulate the presence of this population in housing, education and electoral politics. . . . The 1975 Texas Legislature's attempt to exclude undocumented immigrants from access to K–12 constitutes an example of legislation targeting a select group of the school age population based on their race and national origin while using the fig leaf or immigration status. An analysis from critical race theory points out the fact that given the absence of efforts to target certain undocumented groups, such as Canadians or Irish of European descent, it is race and national origin which is the basis for determining the targets of the legislation. . . .

Economics of Illegal Immigration

Mexican undocumented immigration, has historically served the purposes of the private economic sector in the United States (e.g. agro-business, service industries, the food industry, and increasingly basic industry). The employers, by driving worker's salaries and labor conditions down, create economic sectors largely occupied by immigrant labor. The business sector, taking advantage of these workers' undocumented status and a constant fear of deportation, imposes lower wages, poor working conditions, which they hope will provide them with a more subservient work force.

An economic analysis of the issue must necessarily address the question of resources and their allocation. As pointed out above the State of Texas argued that implementation of 21.031 [The law preventing illegal aliens from getting free public education] was simply a "financial measure designed to avoid a drain on the State's" public treasure. However, in its response, the Supreme Court argued three basic points:

First, the court maintained that although there was a growth in the number of students along the border and major metropolitan areas, "the increase in school enrollment was primarily attributable to the admission of children who were legal residents."

Second, the court pointed out that "...while the exclusion of all undocumented children from the Texas schools would eventually result in economies at some level ... it would not necessarily improve the quality of education."

Education Quality

The Supreme Court's pronouncement regarding educational quality was a response to the fact that school districts opposed to the enrollment of immigrant students maintained that "the enrollment of undocumented children detracts from the quality of educational programs available to citizen children residing in their district."

As a final point to the educational argument, the court later maintained that not educating these children would promote the "creation and perpetuation of a subclass of illiterates within our boundaries, surely adding to the problems and costs of unemployment, welfare and crime. Although this position was formally favorable to the inclusion of undocumented immigrants in public schools, its reasoning is predicated on the view that without an education, these undocumented students would tend to be either unemployed, on welfare or committing crimes. This position borders on characterizing immigrants in pathological terms..."

As it pertained to the argument of economic drain, the high court addressed the issue concluding: "...there is no evidence in the record suggesting that illegal entrants impose any significant burden on the State's economy. To the contrary, the available evidence suggests that illegal aliens underutilize public services, while contributing their labor to the local economy and tax money to the state fisc [public treasury]." This underutilization of public services by the undocumented pointed out by the Supreme Court is determined based on the fact that they are obliged to be taxpayers themselves through sales taxes and the mandatory employer withholding of payroll taxes, even though they are precluded, by their immigration status, from reaping the benefits of such contribution.

New Anti-Immigration Measures

Since the Supreme Court reached its 1982 decision in the *Plyler v. Doe*, there have been two decisions that attempted to overturn that decision. One is Proposition 187, which became law in California in 1994. Its proponents argued: "the multitude of problems facing California—economic recession, social unrest, high crime, environmental degradation—are being caused or aggravated by undocumented immigrants."

At the core of Proposition 187 was the denial of public educational services (K–12) to the undocumented. In addition to denying access to educational and health services, Proposition 187 required that school and health officials report to the INS [Immigration and Naturalization Service] the presence of suspected undocumented immigrants on their premises. This posed the question of what persons, or class of persons, would be subjected to scrutiny as to their citizenship or immigration status, and based upon what assumptions or criteria. Although this initiative was approved during the November 1994 elections in California, it was never enforced due to public outcry and the resistance exercised by various groups such as teachers, and high school immigrants who organized large student walkouts in the Los Angeles metropolitan area.

The similitude between the 1975 Texas legislature provision and the 1994 California ballot initiative is striking. Critical race theory not only allows us to understand that both laws attempted to deny educational services to undocumented students but also, that they unmistakably targeted the Latino population. From this perspective, the anti-immigrant discourse is understood as an attempt at obfuscating the economic interests and racism involved, arguing fiscal burden while implicitly promoting anti-Latino attitudes. The fact that half of the U.S. Latino population resides in Texas and California, with the significant implications for both, may help explain why these initiatives took place in these particular states.

The Debate Continues

The other proposal, not so widely known, was the Gallegly Amendment, which would have allowed states to deny elementary and secondary education to undocumented children. It was initially included in the Immigration Bill (HR 3019) before Congress that became the Illegal Immigration Reform and Immigrant Responsibility Act (IIRIRA) of 1996. Had it succeeded, it would have effectively overturned *Plyler v. Doe.*

While the issue of undocumented students' access to K–12 appears to have been settled in the legal domain for the moment, its enforcement remains the subject of debate. As an example, in September of 2002, a New Jersey school superintendent denied admission to a group of five undocumented children. In an infringement of the *Plyler* decision, the Superintendent not only violated the students' rights by questioning the mothers about their immigration status but also threatened to turn them over to the Immigration and Naturalization Service (INS). This particular case of the Medrano family involves a group of Canadian citizens of Salvadoran descent. From a critical race theory perspective it is pertinent to inquire whether these children's right to a public education would have been denied if they had not been Spanish-speaking Latin American immigrants. As with Proposition 187 in California, those opposed to undocumented immigrants' access to a basic education, use immigration status as a pretext, while targeting students on the basis of their race. In the New Jersey case, the welcome back letter from the Superintendent's office in retraction of the denial shows how cultural differences are used as the fig leaf to justify exclusionary policies: "While *di-*

versity makes conflicts inevitable [italics added], these issues are related to governmental legalities and not to our commitment to all children, *regardless of race and color* [italics added], gender, ethnicity, or origin."

> "As parents labor to pay ever-higher taxes, their children must share their schools with scores of illegal aliens— most not English speaking."

Plyler v. Doe Ignored the Needs of American Taxpayers and Children

Howard Sutherland

In this article, Howard Sutherland argues that William Brennan abused his powers as a Supreme Court justice in order to create a right to education for illegal alien children that is simply not found in the Constitution. According to Sutherland, Brennan based his decision on the due process clause of the Fourteenth Amendment to the Constitution, but ignored the context of that amendment—the need to grant rights to slaves who had been born in the United States. Moreover, Brennan simply disregarded the costs his policy would have for taxpayers and American children. The final point of the article is that the Court has taken power that rightly belongs to Congress, and that Congress can and should take that power back by invalidating rulings such as Plyler. Sutherland is a lawyer in New York and a frequent contributor to vdare.com and frontpagemag.com.

Behind truly insane public policy mandates in the United States, you often find the U.S. Supreme Court, willfully misinterpreting the Constitution to reach the political result favored by a majority of the justices.

The Court Manufactured a Right

Many of the Supreme Court's most overreaching decisions have involved the 14th Amendment. For over 30 years, Justice William Brennan—a New Jersey native—was one of the Court's most inventive and reliably liberal judicial legislators. The "constitutional right" of illegal aliens to public schooling at Americans' expense is one of the many "implied rights" Brennan discovered, hidden deep between the Constitution's inky lines.

He manufactured this novel entitlement in his opinion for narrow a 5–4 majority in *Plyler v. Doe*. *Plyler* has wreaked havoc on public education (and school finances) ever since.

Plyler was a class action suit brought on behalf of Mexican illegal aliens against the State of Texas, the Texas Education Agency and various Texas school districts. In its finding, the Supreme Court struck down a Texas statute withholding from local school districts any state funds for the education of children who were not legally admitted into the United States.

Observers across the country knew that *Plyler* was a critical case. Filing briefs for the illegal alien appellees were the American Immigration Lawyers Association, the American Jewish Committee, the Asian American Legal Defense and Education Fund (briefed by Bill Lann Lee, later President [Bill] Clinton's illegally-appointed head of the Justice Department's Civil Rights Division), the Mexican American Bar Association of Houston, the American Friends Service Committee and the National Education Association.

Incredibly, given the burden *Plyler* would come to impose on Californians, the California State Board Education also filed a brief supporting the illegal aliens.

Weighing in for Texas was a far smaller group, including the Federation for American Immigration Reform.

The reason the Court gave for overturning this perfectly reasonable Texas law was the Equal Protection Clause of the 14th Amendment, which reads:

> No State shall . . . deny to any person within its jurisdiction the equal protection of the laws.

The Court's one-vote majority reached its desired result largely by side-stepping the actual wording of the 14th Amendment and by making assumptions that were both irrelevant to a legal analysis of the Equal Protection Clause and insupportably favorable to illegal aliens.

The Court treated it as a given that most or all of these illegal alien children would wind up staying in the United States and eventually becoming legal residents. That they should be, well, *deported* was never seriously considered.

Neither was the fact that, as citizens of another country, all presumably had a right to whatever education their homelands provide.

The Court Ignored the Content of the 14th Ammendment

After noting—truthfully but pointlessly—that an illegal alien is a "person," Justice Brennan got on with rationalizing his contention that guaranteeing the equal protection of the laws to illegal aliens requires Americans to school their children for free.

But Brennan had a problem to dispose of: While the 14th Amendment's Due Process Clause is unqualified, the Equal Protection Clause applies to "any person within [a State's] jurisdiction."

To attain his desired result, Brennan tossed aside the limiting language about jurisdiction as meaningless—the same way the Federal government misconstrues the 14th Amendment's Citizenship Clause to grant U.S. citizenship to illegal aliens' U.S.-born children. Thus he maintained that the "Equal Protection Clause was intended to work nothing less than the abolition of all caste-based and invidious class-based legislation."

In support Brennan quoted the 14th Amendment's Congressional ratification debates. But he buried their context: These debates were all about prohibiting legal discrimination against freed slaves—Americans, not foreigners whose very presence in a state is a crime. To equate the two is insulting to the former slaves and their descendents. . . .

The Equal Protection Clause does provide a guarantee that, for example, a citizen of Louisiana in Texas is as protected against denials of life, liberty and property—enjoys the same due process of Texas and Federal law—as a Texan. The same would be true of a Mexican national in Texas.

However, even if one believes the 14th Amendment incorporates all of the amendments in the Bill of Rights, applying them against the states as well as the Federal government, the Equal Protection Clause still does not extend to discretionary benefits offered by a state—such as 12 years of very expensive schooling, provided free. . . .

For the majority, . . . Justice Brennan airily, dismissed the Texas law as having means—denial of school funding for illegal aliens—unrelated to its ends of cost control. With that out of the way, he abandoned altogether, the idea that legal admission to the United States, or even American citizenship, should mean anything at all—in favor of a compulsory compassion for the illegal aliens he favors at the expense of the Americans he clearly does not:

> In addition to the pivotal role of education in *sustaining our political and cultural heritage*, [emphasis added] denial of education to some isolated group of children poses an affront to one of the goals of the Equal Protection Clause: the abolition of governmental barriers preventing unreasonable obstacles to advancement on the basis of individual merit. . . . Illiteracy is an enduring disability. The inability to read and write will handicap the individual deprived of a basic education each and every day of his life.

Ignoring the Harm to America

What is striking is the presumption that *America's* political and cultural heritage is somehow sustained by providing free schooling to multitudes of foreign nationals and that it is Americans' constitutional duty to guarantee foreigners' children educational excellence.

The harm done to *American* parents and children was never considered. As parents labor to pay ever-higher taxes, their children must share their schools with scores of illegal aliens—most not English-speaking. Or the parents can take on the double burden of sending their children to private schools.

None of this mattered to Brennan. He asserted that American states must school illegal aliens because denying them access to public schools:

> . . .imposes a lifetime hardship on a discrete class of children not accountable for their disabling status. The stigma of illiteracy will mark them for the rest of their lives. By denying these children a basic education, we deny them the ability *to live within the structure of our civic institutions,* and foreclose any realistic possibility that they will *contribute in even the smallest way to the progress of our Nation.* (emphasis added)

Without using the phrase, the Supreme Court here declared the U.S. a "universal nation," one with no borders—in effect, no nation at all. The only requirement for full participation in American life is to get here—somehow, anyhow.

Justice Brennan's final rationale for the majority's result was the most cynical: the Federal government does next to nothing about removing illegal aliens, so it is tacitly granting them permission to stay. He wrote:

> Sheer incapacity or tax enforcement of the laws barring entry, into this country, coupled with the failure to establish an effective bar to the employment of undocumented [*sic*] aliens, has resulted in the creation of a substantial "shadow

population" of illegal migrants—numbering in the millions—within our borders. . . . To be sure, like all people who have entered the United States unlawfully, [illegal alien] children are subject to deportation. But there is no assurance that a child subject to deportation will ever be deported. An illegal entrant might be granted federal permission to continue to reside in this country, or even to become a citizen. . . . It would of course be most difficult for the State to justify a denial of education to a child *enjoying an inchoate federal permission to remain.* (emphasis added)

Lax Enforcement

This part is Ronald Reagan's fault. The Reagan Administration gave Brennan just the excuse he needed for such an extraordinary assertion when, in 1981, Attorney General William French Smith threw up his hands before the Congress and *admitted* that an impotent administration had no inclination to enforce the immigration laws. . . .

Usurpation of Congressional Powers

Plyler v. Doe is a naked usurpation of Congressional powers—as Chief Justice [Warren] Burger emphasized in his dissent:

> The Court makes no attempt to disguise that it is acting to make up for Congress' lack of "effective leadership" in dealing with the serious national problems caused by the influx of uncountable millions of illegal aliens across our borders. . . . However, it is not the function of the Judiciary to provide "effective leadership simply because the political branches of government fail to do so. . . . The Court employs, and in my view, abuses the Fourteenth Amendment in an effort to become an omnipotent and omniscient problem solver. That the motives for doing so are noble and compassionate does not alter the fact that the Court distorts our constitutional function to make amends for the defaults of others. . . . If ever a court was guilty of an unabashedly result-oriented approach, this case is a prime example.

The last sentence of the Chief Justice's dissent sums up:

> The solution to this seemingly intractable problem is to defer to the political processes, unpalatable as that may be to some.

The answer to *Plyler* is political. The 14th Amendment itself says "the Congress shall have the power to enforce, by appropriate legislation, the provisions of this article." Contrary to what most people today believe, the Supreme Court is not the sole interpreter of the Constitution. The Congress can and should pass legislation clarifying that the Equal Protection Clause cannot be construed to compel a state to provide discretionary benefits, including public education, to anyone who is not legally admitted into the United States. The legislation should *specify that it is not subject to judicial review.*

At one stroke, such a law would overturn *Plyler v. Doe*—and go a long way toward countering the growing belief that we have no choice but to pretend that illegal aliens are in fact American citizens.

CHAPTER 4

Extending Civil Rights to Undeportable Aliens

Case Overview

Zadvydas v. Davis (2001)

Most criminal aliens are deported back to their home countries, either immediately on conviction or after serving time in U.S. prisons. There are occasions, however, when an immigrant convicted of a serious crime cannot be deported, such as when there are no political relations between the United States and the home country, or when no foreign citizenship can be established for the criminal. In such cases, it had been the practice in some instances to detain the person indefinitely while working out deportation arrangements. Civil rights and immigrant advocacy groups believed this was unconstitutional, and the cases of Kestutis Zadvydas and Kim Ho Ma became an opportunity to challenge the Immigration and Naturalization Service (INS) practice of indefinite detention.

Kestutis Zadvydas was born in a displaced persons camp in Germany in the aftermath of World War II. Brought to the United States as a child, Zadvydas became a career criminal. When the United States sought to deport him, neither Germany nor Lithuania, his parents' homeland, would accept him as a citizen. Kim Ho Ma left Cambodia at age two and eventually settled in the United States with his parents. He was involved in gang-related violence and the INS took him into custody. As there was no reparation agreement with Cambodia, the agency was unable to send him to that country. He too was placed in indefinite detention.

The two cases were challenged on constitutional grounds under the doctrine of habeas corpus, the idea that persons cannot be held indefinitely without trial. Supreme Court Justice Stephen Breyer, writing for the majority, held that indefinite detention did indeed violate this doctrine. If the INS (the relevant agency is now called Immigration and Customs Enforcement or ICE) could not show that it had a reasonable possibility of deporting the alien, he or she must be released under supervision. Breyer set a limit of 90 days for the government to remove the alien from the United States, after which time it was required to either prove it had a reasonable likelihood of obtaining a deportation arrangement or release the alien.

Justice Anthony Kennedy disagreed strongly with the majority opinion. He wrote that in the age of terrorism, it was folly to force the release of potentially dangerous aliens. Community safety trumped the rights of criminal immigrants, who as foreigners were not entitled to the same rights as U.S. citizens. Moreover, the 90-day limit on detention gave both criminal aliens and uncooperative foreign governments an incentive to delay the repatriation process in the hopes of "running out the clock" and winning a release back into American society.

The danger of potential terrorism from former INS (and ICE) detainees has come to the forefront in the post-9/11 age. (*Zadvydas* was decided in the winter before the World Trade Center and Pentagon attacks.) The effect of the decision, however, might not have been as profound as Justice Kennedy feared, as federal agencies appeared to respond by redoubling their efforts to remove criminal aliens by bringing strong pressure against uncooperative foreign governments.

> "A statute permitting indefinite deten-
> tion of an alien would raise a serious
> constitutional problem."

The Court's Decision: Immigration Officials Cannot Detain Undeportable Criminal Aliens Indefinitely

Stephen Breyer

*Sometimes countries refuse to take its citizens back, leaving fed-
eral immigration officials facing a dilemma. This is especially
true in the case of criminal aliens who might pose a danger to
society. Under the U.S. Constitution, persons normally cannot be
held indefinitely without a trial. This right, which is derived
from the habeas corpus provisions of America's basic law, was
claimed by two criminal aliens who were subject to indefinite
detention while awaiting the unlikely event that their home
countries would agree to accept them. The Supreme Court majority agreed that the aliens had the right to be released from detention. Justice Stephen Breyer wrote that federal courts have the
right to review such cases, and, if there is no reasonable likelihood that an alien will be deported, the alien should be set free,
though he or she could be subject to supervision.*

*Breyer is an associate justice of the Supreme Court, ap-
pointed by President Bill Clinton in 1994. He is known as a
pragmatic liberal.*

Stephen Breyer, majority opinion, *Zadvydas v. Davis*, No. 99–7791, *United States Supreme Court of Appeals for the Fifth Circuit*, February 21, 2001.

We consider two separate instances of detention. The first concerns Kestutis Zadvydas, a resident alien who was born, apparently of Lithuanian parents, in a displaced persons camp in Germany in 1948. When he was eight years old, Zadvydas immigrated to the United States with his parents and other family members, and he has lived here ever since.

Zadvydas has a long criminal record, involving drug crimes, attempted robbery, attempted burglary, and theft. He has a history of flight, from both criminal and deportation proceedings. Most recently, he was convicted of possessing, with intent to distribute, cocaine; sentenced to 16 years imprisonment; released on parole after two years; taken into INS [Immigration and Naturalization Service] custody; and, in 1994, ordered deported to Germany.

Two Cases of Indefinite Detention

In 1994, Germany told the INS that it would not accept Zadvydas because he was not a German citizen. Shortly thereafter, Lithuania refused to accept Zadvydas because he was neither a Lithuanian citizen nor a permanent resident. In 1996, the INS asked the Dominican Republic (Zadvydas' wife's country) to accept him, but this effort proved unsuccessful. In 1998, Lithuania rejected, as inadequately documented, Zadvydas' effort to obtain Lithuanian citizenship based on his parents' citizenship; Zadvydas' reapplication is apparently still pending.

The INS kept Zadvydas in custody after expiration of the removal period. In September 1995, Zadvydas filed a petition for a writ of habeas corpus ... challenging his continued detention. In October 1997, a Federal District Court granted that writ and ordered him released under supervision. In its view, the Government would never succeed in its efforts to remove Zadvydas from the United States, leading to his permanent confinement, contrary to the Constitution.

The Fifth Circuit reversed this decision concluded that Zadvydas' detention did not violate the Constitution because eventual deportation was not "impossible," good faith efforts to remove him from the United States continued, and his detention was subject to periodic administrative review. The Fifth Circuit stayed its mandate pending potential review in this Court.

The second case is that of Kim Ho Ma. Ma was born in Cambodia in 1977. When he was two, his family fled, taking him to refugee camps in Thailand and the Philippines and eventually to the United States, where he has lived as a resident alien since the age of seven. In 1995, at age 17, Ma was involved in a gang-related shooting, convicted of manslaughter, and sentenced to 38 months' imprisonment. He served two years, after which he was released into INS custody.

In light of his conviction of an "aggravated felony," Ma was ordered removed. The 90-day removal period expired in early 1999, but the INS continued to keep Ma in custody, because, in light of his former gang membership, the nature of his crime, and his planned participation in a prison hunger strike, it was "unable to conclude that Mr. Ma would remain nonviolent and not violate the conditions of release." . . .

Zadvydas asked us to review the decision of the Fifth Circuit authorizing his continued detention. The Government asked us to review the decision of the Ninth Circuit forbidding Ma's continued detention. We granted writs in both cases, agreeing to consider both statutory and related constitutional questions. We consolidated the two cases for argument; and we now decide them together. . . .

A Serious Constitutional Problem

A statute permitting indefinite detention of an alien would raise a serious constitutional problem. The Fifth Amendment's Due Process Clause forbids the Government to "depriv[e]" any "person . . . of . . . liberty . . . without due process of law." Freedom from imprisonment—from government custody, detention, or other forms of physical restraint—lies at the heart of the liberty that Clause protects. And this Court has said that government detention violates that Clause unless the detention is ordered in a *criminal* proceeding with adequate procedural protections, or, in certain special and "narrow" nonpunitive "circumstances," where a special justification, such as harm-threatening mental illness, outweighs the "individual's constitutionally protected interest in avoiding physical restraint." The proceedings at issue here are civil, not criminal, and we assume that they are nonpunitive in purpose and effect. There is no sufficiently strong special justification here for indefinite civil detention—at least as administered under this statute. The statute, says the Government, has two regulatory goals: "ensuring the appearance of aliens at future immigration proceedings" and "[p]reventing danger to the community." But by definition the first justification—preventing flight—is weak or nonexistent where removal seems a remote possibility at best. . . .

The second justification—protecting the community— does not necessarily diminish in force over time. But we have upheld preventive detention based on dangerousness only when limited to specially dangerous individuals and subject to strong procedural protections. . . . In cases in which preventive detention is of potentially *indefinite* duration, we have also demanded that the dangerousness rationale be accompanied by some other special circumstance, such as mental illness, that helps to create the danger. . . .

Unclear Intent from Congress

Despite this constitutional problem, if "Congress has made its intent" in the statute "clear, 'we must give effect to that intent.'" We cannot find here, however, any clear indication of congressional intent to grant the Attorney General the power to hold indefinitely in confinement an alien ordered removed. And that is so whether protecting the community from dangerous aliens is a primary or (as we believe) secondary statutory purpose. After all, the provision is part of a statute that has as its basic purpose effectuating an alien's removal. Why should we assume that Congress saw the alien's dangerousness as unrelated to this purpose?

The Government points to the statute's word "may." But while "may" suggests discretion, it does not necessarily suggest unlimited discretion. In that respect the word "may" is ambiguous. Indeed, if Congress had meant to authorize long-term detention of unremovable aliens, it certainly could have spoken in clearer terms. The Government points to similar related statutes that *require* detention of criminal aliens during removal proceedings and the removal period, and argues that these show that mandatory detention is the rule while discretionary release is the narrow exception. But the statute before us applies not only to terrorists and criminals, but also to ordinary visa violators, and, more importantly, post-removal-period detention, unlike detention pending a determination of removability or during the subsequent 90-day removal period, has no obvious termination point.

History of Alien Detention

The Government also points to the statute's history. That history catalogs a series of changes, from an initial period (before 1952) when lower courts had interpreted statutory silence, to mean that deportation-related detention must end within a reasonable time, to a period (from the early 1950's through the late 1980's) when the statutes permitted, but did not require, post-deportation-order detention for up to six months, to more recent statutes that have at times mandated and at other times permitted the post-deportation-order detention of aliens falling into certain categories such its aggravated felons.

In early 1996, Congress explicitly expanded the group of aliens subject to mandatory detention, eliminating provisions that permitted release of criminal aliens who had at one time been lawfully admitted to the United States. And later that year Congress enacted the present law, which liberalizes pre-existing law by shortening the removal period from six months to 90 days, mandates detention of certain criminal aliens during the removal proceedings and for the subsequent 90-day removal period, and adds the post-removal-period provision here at issue.

We have found nothing in the history of these statutes that clearly demonstrates a congressional intent to authorize indefinite, perhaps permanent, detention. Consequently, interpreting the statute to avoid a serious constitutional threat, we conclude that, once removal is no longer reasonable foreseeable, continued detention is no longer authorized by statute. . . .

Judicial Review Applies

We recognize, as the Government points out, that review must take appropriate account of the greater immigration-related expertise of the Executive Branch, of the serious administrative needs and concerns inherent in the necessarily extensive INS efforts to enforce this complex statute, and the Nation's need to "speak with one voice" in immigration matters. But we believe that courts can take appropriate account of such matters without abdicating their legal responsibility to review the lawfulness of an alien's continued detention.

Ordinary principles of judicial review in this area recognize primary Executive Branch responsibility. They counsel judges to give expert agencies decision-making leeway in matters that invoke their expertise. They recognize Executive Branch primacy in foreign policy matters. And they consequently require courts to listen with care when the Government's foreign policy judgments, including, for example, the status of repatriation negotiations, are at issue, and to grant the Government appropriate leeway when its judgments rest upon foreign policy expertise.

We realize that recognizing this necessary Executive leeway will often call for difficult judgments. In order to limit the occasions when courts will need to make them, we think it practically necessary to recognize some presumptively reasonable period of detention. We have adopted similar presumptions in other contexts to guide lower court determinations.

Likelihood of Removal Is Key

While an argument can be made for confining any presumption to 90 days, we doubt that when Congress shortened the removal period to 90 days in 1996 it believed that all reasonably foreseeable removals could be accomplished in that time. We do have reason to believe, however, that Congress previously doubted the constitutionality of detention for more than six months. Consequently, for the sake of uniform administration in the federal courts, we recognize that period. After this 6-month period, once the alien provides good reason to believe that there is no significant likelihood of removal in the reasonably foreseeable future, the Government must respond with evidence sufficient to rebut that showing. And for detention to remain reasonable, as the period of prior post-removal confinement grows, what counts as the "reasonably foreseeable future" conversely would have to shrink. This 6-month presumption, of course, does not mean that every alien not removed must be released after six months. To the contrary, an alien may be held in confinement until it has been determined that there is no significant likelihood of removal in the reasonably foreseeable future.

The Fifth Circuit held Zadvydas' continued detention lawful as long as "good faith efforts to effectuate . . . deportation continue" and Zadvydas failed to show that deportation will prove "impossible." But this standard would seem to require an alien seeking release to show the absence of *any* prospect of removal—no matter how unlikely or unforeseeable—which demands more than our reading of the statute can bear. The

Ninth Circuit held that the Government was required to release Ma from detention because there was no reasonable likelihood of his removal in the foreseeable future. But its conclusion may have rested solely upon the "absence" of an "extant or pending" repatriation agreement without giving due weight to the likelihood of successful future negotiations. Consequently, we vacate the decisions below and remand both cases for further proceedings consistent with this opinion.

> "The risk to the community posed by
> the mandatory release of aliens who
> are dangerous or a flight risk is far from
> insubstantial."

Dissenting Opinion: The Court Overstepped Its Bounds in Mandating the Release of Criminal Aliens

Anthony Kennedy

Appointed to the Supreme Court in 1988 by President Ronald Reagan, Anthony Kennedy is considered a moderate, "swing vote" on the Court. In this dissent, Kennedy takes the majority to task for ignoring Congress's intent in the Immigration and Nationality Act, specifically the sections of the law regarding deportable aliens. The justices ignore the plain text of the law, according to Kennedy, instead substituting their own invention of a six-month period during which a criminal alien must be deported or released. This ruling is counterproductive because it weakens the U.S. government's hand when negotiating with foreign powers over the return of its citizens, encourages aliens in detention to delay procedures in the hopes of reaching the six months' maximum in confinement, and exposes the community to risk from deportable criminals who now must be released.

The Court says its duty is to avoid a constitutional question. It deems the duty performed by interpreting a statute in obvious disregard of congressional intent; curing the

Anthony Kennedy, dissenting opinion, *Zadvydas v. Davis*, No. 99–7791, *United States Supreme Court of Appeals for the Fifth Circuit*, February 21, 2001.

resulting gap by writing a statutory amendment of its own; committing its own grave constitutional error by arrogating to the Judicial Branch the power to summon high officers of the Executive to assess their progress in conducting some of the Nation's most sensitive negotiations with foreign powers; and then likely releasing into our general population at least hundreds of removable or inadmissible aliens who have been found by fair procedures to be flight risks, dangers to the community, or both. Far from avoiding a constitutional question, the Court's ruling causes systemic dislocation in the balance of powers, thus raising serious constitutional concerns not just for the cases at hand but for the Court's own view of its proper authority. Any supposed respect the Court seeks in not reaching the constitutional question is outweighed by the intrusive and erroneous exercise of its own powers. In the guise of judicial restraint the Court ought not to intrude upon the other branches. The constitutional question the statute presents, it must be acknowledged, may be a significant one in some later case; but it ought not to drive us to an incorrect interpretation of the statute. The Court having reached the wrong result for the wrong reason, this respectful dissent is required.

The Immigration Law Is Straightforward

The Immigration and Nationality Act (INA), is straightforward enough. It provides:

> An alien ordered removed who is inadmissible under section 1182 of this title, removable under section 1227(a)(1)(C), 1227(a)(2) or 1227(a)(4) [various sections of the INA] of this title or who has been determined by the Attorney General to be a risk to the community or unlikely to comply with the order of removal, may be detained beyond the removal period and, if released, shall be subject to the terms of supervision in paragraph.

By this statute, Congress confers upon the Attorney General discretion to detain an alien ordered removed. It gives express authorization to detain "beyond the removal period." The class of removed aliens detainable under the section includes aliens who were inadmissible and aliens subject to final orders of removal, provided they are a risk to the community or likely to flee. The issue to be determined is whether the authorization to detain beyond the removal period is subject to the implied, nontextual limitation that the detention be no longer than reasonably necessary to effect removal to another country. . . .

Putting the Community at Risk

The 6-month period invented by the Court, even when modified by its sliding standard of reasonableness for certain repatriation negotiations, makes the statutory purpose to protect the community ineffective. The risk to the community exists whether or not the repatriation negotiations have some end in sight; in fact, when the negotiations end, the risk may be greater. The authority to detain beyond the removal period is to protect the community, not to negotiate the aliens' return. The risk to the community survives repatriation negotiations. To a more limited, but still significant, extent, so does the concern with flight. It is a fact of international diplomacy that governments and their policies change; and if repatriation efforts can be revived, the Attorney General has an interest in ensuring the alien can report so the removal process can begin again.

The majority's unanchored interpretation ignores another indication that the Attorney General's detention discretion was not limited to this truncated period. Section 1231(a)(6) permits continued detention not only of removable aliens but also of inadmissible aliens, for instance those stopped at the border before entry. Congress provides for detention of both categories within the same statutory grant of authority. Accepting the majority's interpretation, then, there are two possibilities, neither of which is sustainable. On the one hand, it may be that the majority's rule applies to both categories of aliens, in which case we are asked to assume that Congress intended to restrict the discretion it could confer upon the Attorney General so that all inadmissible aliens must be allowed into our community within six months. On the other hand, the majority's logic might be that inadmissible and removable aliens can be treated differently. Yet it is not a plausible construction of [Section] 1231(a)(6) to imply a time limit as to one class but not to another. The text does not admit of this possibility. As a result, it is difficult to see why [the majority states] "[a]liens who have not yet gained initial admission to this country would present a very different question."

Congress' power to detain aliens in connection with removal or exclusion, the Court has said, is part of the Legislature's considerable authority over immigration matters. It is reasonable to assume, then, and it is the proper interpretation of the INA and [Section] 1231(a)(6), that when Congress provided for detention "beyond the removal period," it exercised its considerable power over immigration and delegated to the Attorney General the discretion to detain inadmissible and other removable aliens for as long as they are determined to be either a flight risk or a danger to the Nation.

Repatriation Now More Difficult

The majority's interpretation, moreover, defeats the very repatriation goal in which it professes such interest. The Court rushes to substitute a judicial judgment for the Executive's discretion and authority. As the Government represents to us, judicial orders requiring release of removable aliens, even on a temporary basis, have the potential to undermine the obvious necessity that the Nation speak with one voice on immigration and foreign affairs matters. The result of the Court's rule is that, by refusing to accept repatriation of their own nationals, other countries can effect the release of these individuals back into the American community. If their own nationals are now at large in the United States, the nation of origin may ignore or disclaim responsibility to accept their return. The interference with sensitive foreign relations becomes even more acute where hostility or tension characterizes the relationship, for other countries can use the fact of judicially mandated release to their strategic advantage, refusing the return of their nationals to force dangerous aliens upon us. One of the more alarming aspects of the Court's new venture into foreign affairs management is the suggestion that the district court can expand or contract the reasonable period of detention based on its own assessment of the course of negotiations with foreign powers. The Court says it will allow the Executive to perform its duties on its own for six months; after that, foreign relations go into judicially supervised receivership. . . .

It is to be expected that from time to time a foreign power will adopt a truculent stance with respect to the United States and other nations. Yet the Court by its time limit, or presumptive time limit, goes far to undercut the position of the Executive in repatriation negotiations, thus ill serving the interest of all foreign nationals of the country concerned. Law-abiding aliens might wish to return to their home country, for instance, but the strained relationship caused by the difficult repatriation talks might prove to be a substantial obstacle for these aliens as well.

In addition to weakening the hand of our Government, court ordered release cannot help but encourage dilatory and obstructive tactics by aliens who, emboldened by the Court's new rule, have good reason not to cooperate by making their own repatriation or transfer seem foreseeable. An alien ordered deported also has less incentive to cooperate or to facilitate expeditious removal when he has been released, even on a supervised basis, than does an alien held at an Immigration and Naturalization Service (INS) detention facility. Neither the alien nor his family would find any urgency in assisting with a petition to other countries to accept the alien back if the alien could simply remain in the United States indefinitely.

Danger May Remain After Prison

The risk to the community posed by the mandatory release of aliens who are dangerous or a flight risk is far from insubstantial; the motivation to protect the citizenry from aliens determined to be dangerous is central to the immigration power itself. The Government statistical studies showing high recidivism rates for released aliens. One Government Accounting Office study cited by Congress in floor debates on the Antiterrorism and Effective Death Penalty Act of 1996, put the figure as high as 77 percent. It seems evident a criminal record accumulated by an admitted alien during his or her time in the United States is likely to be a better indicator of risk than factors relied upon during the INS's initial decision to admit or exclude. Aliens ordered deported as the result of having committed a felony have proved to be dangerous.

Any suggestion that aliens who have completed prison terms no longer present a danger simply does not accord with the reality that a significant risk may still exist, as determined by the many factors set forth in the regulations. Underworld and terrorist links are subtle and may be overseas, beyond our jurisdiction to impose felony charges. Furthermore, the majority's rationale seems to apply to an alien who flees prosecution or escapes from custody in some other country. The fact an alien can be deemed inadmissible because of fraud at the time of entry does not necessarily distinguish his or her case from an alien whose entry was legal. Consider, for example, a fugitive alien who enters by fraud or stealth and resides here for five years with significant ties to the community, though still presenting a danger; contrast him with an alien who entered lawfully but a month later committed an act making him removable. Why the Court's rationale should apply to the second alien but not the first is not apparent.

> "[Zadvydas] *may be used as a tool for enemy nations to force their dangerous criminals, terrorists even, onto our shores and into our cities."*

The *Zadvydas* Decision Allows Potential Terrrorists to Live at Large in the United States

Christopher Sheridan

In this commentary on the Zadvydas *case, Christopher Sheridan makes the case that the decision endangers public safety in the United States. He believes this has already been shown in the case of ordinary criminal refugees, who having served time in U.S. prisons, were released into society rather than being deported or detained while awaiting deportation. Sheridan finds the situation more critical today, after 9/11, with hundreds of Taliban and al Qaeda terrorists in U.S. custody undergoing trial. American officials will have difficulty deporting many of these prisoners after their sentences are served, as their home nations will not wish to accept convicted terrorists. Sheridan raises the spector of Islamic militants being loosed on the streets, extending their networks into the heart of America's cities and towns. Sheridan is a graduate of the Whittier Law School.*

Before oral arguments were heard in *Zadvydas*, an amicus brief (WLF Brief) was filed by the Washington Legal Foundation (WLF) and the Allied Educational Foundation in support of the respondents, addressing the potential adverse

Christopher Sheridan, "*Zadvydas v. Davis*: The Judicial Parole Program for Dangerous Criminal Aliens," *Whittier Law Review*, vol. 24, 2002, pp. 351–357. Copyright © 2002 Whittier Law School. All rights reserved. Reproduced by permission.

effects the case could have on society. The WLF Brief stated that Mr. Zadvydas's case could not "be decided in a vacuum. The decision in this case is likely to affect hundreds if not thousands of cases involving criminal aliens who are subject to final deportation/removal orders but whose removal, for a variety of reasons, cannot be effected in the immediate future." The WLF Brief went on to state that the impact would be most pronounced in the Ninth Circuit as a result of its decision in *Ma v. Reno*. As of the date the WLF Brief was filed, "the INS [Immigration and Naturalization Service] had appeals pending in fifty-nine Ninth Circuit cases in which criminal aliens had been ordered released."

> Moreover, as of that date there were 400 other cases raising similar challenges to detention in various district courts in the Ninth Circuit. . . . One can expect that each of those criminal aliens will be released from detention, as will numerous other criminal aliens in each of the other circuits, if the Court upholds Mr. Zadvydas's substantive due process claims.

Justice [Anthony] Kennedy shared WLF's concern that hundreds of dangerous criminal aliens may be set free, and so he provided the following upsetting example in his dissent:

> An example is presented in the case of Saroeut Ourk, a Cambodian alien determined to be removable and held pending deportation. . . . Ourk was convicted of rape by use of drugs in conjunction with the kidnapping of a [thirteen]-year-old girl; after serving [eighteen] months of his prison term, he was released on parole but was returned to custody twice more for parole violations. . . . When he was ordered deported and transferred to the custody of the INS, it is no surprise the INS determined he was both a flight risk and a danger to the community. Yet the Court of Appeals for the Ninth Circuit concluded, based on its earlier decision in *Kim Ho Ma v. Reno*, . . . that Ourk could no longer be held pending deportation, since removal to Cambodia was not reasonably foreseeable. . . .

The Ninth Circuit's release of these dangerous criminal aliens back into society is, unfortunately, just the tip of the iceberg, as the Court's holding in *Zadvydas* is now the law across the United States. Many lower courts have begun to apply *Zadvydas*, thereby effectuating the release into society of dangerous removable criminal aliens across this country.

[In 2002] there are about three hundred suspected Taliban and al Qaeda [terrorist group] members being detained and interrogated by the United States military at the American naval base at Guantanamo Bay, Cuba. In probably the scariest and most perverse consequence of the majority's holding in *Zadvydas*, those terrorist detainees could someday be released into the United States. How this nightmarish result could be realized is explained in Justice Kennedy's dissent.

> The majority's rule is not limited to aliens once lawfully admitted. Today's result may well mandate the release of those aliens who first gained entry illegally or by fraud, and, indeed, is broad enough to require even that inadmissible and excludable aliens detained at the border ... be set free in our community.

By means of illustration Justice Kennedy pointed to *Rosales-Garcia v. Holland*, a case concerning a Cuban citizen who arrived in the 1980 Mariel Boatlift. Rosales, an inadmissible alien, was released into the United States "under the Attorney General's authority to parole illegal aliens, ... and there he committed multiple crimes [such as burglary, grand larceny and even prison escape] for which he was convicted and imprisoned." Rosales's immigration parole was revoked and he was detained and ordered deported. Justice Kennedy stated:

> In reasoning remarkably similar to the majority's, the Court of Appeals for the Sixth Circuit held that the indefinite detention of Rosales violated Fifth Amendment due process rights, because "the government offered ... no credible

proof that there is any possibility that Cuba may accept Rosales's return anytime in the foreseeable future." ... This result—that Mariel Cubans and other illegal, inadmissible aliens will be released notwithstanding their criminal history and obvious flight risk—would seem a necessary consequence of the majority's construction of the statute.

Justice Kennedy could not have been more accurate. Just a few months after *Zadvydas* was decided, the United States District Court for the District of Minnesota decided *Borrero v. Aljets*. *Borrero* is a typical case in which a Mariel Boatlift Cuban, released on immigration parole, who committed many crimes—robbery, theft, drug possession, felon in possession of a pistol—served his time, had his parole revoked, was ordered deported, and was detained by the INS.

Judge Noel, from the United States District Court, recommended that Borrero be granted *habeas corpus* relief and be released. His recommendation was based on his ten-page opinion, which relied exclusively on *Zadvydas* for support of the proposition that Borrero's Fifth amendment rights were being violated. . . .

If *Zadvydas* can be used by the lower courts to grant release to even an excludable/inadmissible alien then there truly is no class of alien left who can be detained by the INS beyond six months, provided [Justice Stephen Breyer wrote] "that there is no significant likelihood of removal in the reasonably foreseeable future." Now, consider for a moment how easily this concept can be applied to the Taliban and al Qaeda members at Guantanamo. . . .

First, they must complete their sentence at Guantanamo or elsewhere for whatever terrorist or war crimes of which they can be convicted. If they are not given life sentences, then upon their release the INS will detain them and order them deported. Then certainly due to their reputation as terrorists, these men will find it extraordinarily difficult to find a country to accept them (or that the United States will approve their extradition to; i.e. not Iraq, Iran, or other terrorist friendly states) so they will remain in INS detention for a reasonable time of six months. The next step is to file for a writ of *habeas corpus*, and have it approved under *Zadvydas* because the government will be unable to rebut the fact that there is no significant likelihood of removal. Finally, the last step in the *Zadvydas* majority's judicial parole program, is for the more than three hundred Taliban and al Qaeda members to be released into the United States community (just as hundreds of other criminal aliens have been, beginning with the Ninth Circuit's *Ma* decision) where they can begin to take up the meaningful activities common to other visiting aliens— such as attending flight school.

All dark humor aside, the above scenario is very scary and it is also a very real possibility under the Court's ruling in *Zadvydas*. Faced with this perverse consequence, Justice Scalia's brief dissenting opinion looks all the more attractive because the Guantanamo detainees, and all other removable aliens would not have any constitutional right to release in this country.

Zadvydas was, at the time it was decided, merely an odd result and a bad decision on the part of the five justices who participated in the majority. It reflected a sympathetic desire on their part to see that all aliens who have been ordered removed, are not left to languish forever in INS detention facilities with no hope of finding a country to accept them. But since September 11, [2001] the case has taken on the greater dimensions than Justice Kennedy foresaw. The case may be used as a tool for enemy nations to force their dangerous criminals, terrorists even, onto our shores and into our cities regardless if they are stopped at the border.

Justice Kennedy stated, "Underworld and terrorist links are subtle and may be overseas." September 11 proved Justice Kennedy's statement beyond a shadow of a doubt when, from thousands of miles away in Afghanistan, Osama Bin Laden was able to orchestrate the murderous actions of nineteen men in the United States. Some of those terrorist men were not in this country legally. Prior to the *Zadvydas* decision, America had a fighting chance against them. Had they been discovered they could have been detained until their removal from this country. *Zadvydas* changed all that. It stripped away the ability of the INS and the Attorney General to exercise their discretion to detain dangerous criminal aliens. Now, the detention of terrorist aliens is nothing more than a six-month delay in their plans, and terrorists are patient.

Post-9/11 Legislation Has Stymied the Increased Rights for Immigrants Promised by *Zadvydas*

N. Alejandra Arroyave

In this article, N. Alejandra Arroyave argues that the potential for increasing immigrants' rights after the Zadvydas decision has been stymied after the terrorist attacks on the World Trade Center and the Pentagon on September 11, 2001. Since that time legislation, especially the USA Patriot Act, has expanded the federal government's ability to detain immigrants. The Court's ruling contained an exception for "special circumstances" and the executive branch has used this language to justify expanded detensions of some aliens. In a sense the Zadvydas decision is being turned on its head by the new climate of fear in the post-9/11 era. Arroyave is a 2003 graduate of the University of Miami School of Law.

After a long history of denying constitutional protections to aliens under the guise of the plenary power doctrine, *Zadvydas* is a breakthrough decision within the Supreme Court's immigration jurisprudence. Deemed the first in a

N. Alejandra Arroyave, "Preserving the Essence of *Zadvydas v. Davis* in the Midst of a National Tragedy," *University of Miami Law Review*, vol. 57, 2002–2003, pp. 251–254, 256–258. Reproduced by permission.

"new era of immigrants' rights," the Court effectively discarded the strongest arguments for limiting constitutional protections of aliens that had been justified by Congress's plenary power to detain immigrants indefinitely. For the first time, the Supreme Court acknowledged that noncitizens are entitled to the same protections as citizens. After the Court's ruling on June 28, 2001, the Immigration and Naturalization Service (INS) reported that 3,399 detainees could be eligible for release under the new six-month reasonably foreseeable standard. Hundreds of potential beneficiaries of *Zadvydas* included detainees from countries that lacked repatriation agreements with the United States, such as Cuba, Laos, Cambodia, and Vietnam.

While the *Zadvydas* decision provided renewed optimism for many detainees, September 11, 2001, clouded any hope for a promising new chapter within immigration law. The terrorist attack on the World Trade Center and the Pentagon was not only an attack on United States soil, but also an attack on the psyche of the American people. A distortion of religious views led aliens from the Middle East to commit suicide attacks, killing Americans and citizens from many parts of the world. Hours after the tragedy, the American people first learned that the lives of innocent victims had been irrationally sacrificed because of foreign-based animosity towards the United States. That moment sparked a renewed cycle in anti-immigrant sentiment, leading to widespread paranoia that will perhaps curb any progress that *Zadvydas* achieved within the aliens' rights tradition.

Exceptions to the Riding Against Indefinite Detention

In the aftermath of September 11, and in the subsequent debate on civil rights, *Zadvydas* is regarded as prophetic because many of the concerns elucidated in the opinion reflect the current debate on aliens' rights versus national security. The majority opinion contains language that can be construed as an exception to the Court's reasonably foreseeable six-month standard. For example, while condemning the potential erosion of civil rights due to the indefinite detention of deportable aliens, the Court clarified that its decision was not necessarily applicable in "special circumstances." Explicitly referring to terrorism, the Court acknowledged that deference must be given to the political branches in matters involving foreign policy and national security. "Neither do we consider terrorism or other special circumstances where special arguments might be made for forms of preventive detention and for heightened deference to the judgments of the political branches with respect to matters of national security." In an opinion upholding the constitutional rights of aliens to be free from indefinite detention, this language can be considered simple dicta [mere opinion] or an exception to the rule against indefinite detention. The current national tension and the war on terrorism, however, might permit this exception to swallow the rule, and allow *Zadvydas* to be viewed as a case which actually justifies the Government instead of condemning it in affording less due process rights to aliens. While the new measures proposed and adopted by Congress and the INS are necessary to combat terrorist threats by American enemies, the measures will most likely circumvent any progress achieved within the aliens' rights tradition at the expense of innocent, non-terrorist aliens.

Power to Detain Aliens Expands After 9/11

On October 26, 2001, President George W. Bush signed into law the Uniting and Strengthening America by Providing Appropriate Tools Required to Intercept and Obstruct Terrorism Act (USA PATRIOT Act). Among many budgetary and statutory changes that will help prevent future terrorist acts, Congress amended the INA to heighten enforcement of immigration violations. Through section 412 of the USA PATRIOT

Act, Congress added section 236A to the INA [Immigration and Nationality Act], entitled "Mandatory Detention of Suspected Terrorists; Habeas Corpus; Judicial Review." Under the new section 236A, Congress granted the Attorney General the power to detain any alien whom he certifies is a suspected terrorist. Certification occurs if the Attorney General has "reasonable grounds to believe" that an alien is a security threat or terrorist as already defined in the Act. Furthermore, the Attorney General must bring charges against an alien within seven days after detention, allowing release if the procedural rule is not followed. This provision expands the power to detain, as the previous rule required that the alien be charged within forty-eight hours after detention.

Most notable, however, is the language in the new section 236A concerning indefinite detention. Under the new section 236A, the Attorney General is allowed to detain an alien beyond the ninety-day statutory detention period for removal. The section incorporates the "reasonably foreseeable" standard implemented by the *Zadvydas* Court, but in such a way that it actually allows the Attorney General to detain indefinitely "only if the release of an alien will threaten the national security of the United States or the safety of the community or any person." The Act permits the Attorney General discretion to review an alien's case every six months and revoke certification. The text of the new section implements the Court's new standard, yet also implements a distorted view of the decision based on a narrow interpretation of *Zadvydas*. . . .

Public Reaction

While the new measures, encouraged by the USA Patriot Act . . . find justification within the language of *Zadvydas*, experts and the media have labeled the measures employed by the authorities since September 11 to be the "antithesis of due process." Proponents of the measures, however, claim that the regulations have not undermined the progressive effect of the *Zadvydas* decision. The Service reported that since *Zadvydas* and even since September 11, the Service has released detainees from Iran, Iraq, Afghanistan, and Jordan. According to the Service, these detainees proved that they would not pose a threat to public safety and would comply with surveillance conditions. Other proponents argue that the new measures do not actually deal with the issue of indefinite detention as reviewed by the Supreme Court. The regulations merely allow the Government to revoke the bond of a dangerous alien during the ninety-day removal period, which was not at issue *Zadvydas*. The measures do not allow detention beyond the ninety-day statutory period or beyond any six-month reasonably foreseeable period. Referring to the exceptions mentioned in *Zadvydas*, proponents argue that such measures are "well within the bounds of constitutionality."

Attorney General John Ashcroft [who left the office in 2005] has attempted to dismiss any criticism offered by civil rights advocates. According to Ashcroft, critics have overstated the role that the new measures might play in eroding civil rights. The Attorney General has assured that the new measures reflect a meditated, balance between security and rights. Using the now infamous discourse on the war against terrorism, Ashcroft accused critics of the new regulations of aiding terrorists by figuratively supplying enemies with "ammunition" to "erode our national unity and diminish our resolve." The Attorney General finds validation for the new measures in a terrorist manual that instructs its members to use American liberties against America. Ashcroft claims that measures allowing secrecy in proceedings and extended detention are necessary to prevent communication among terrorist networks. Any leeway given in these proceedings is considered by the administration to be a lost battle in the war against terrorism.

Detentions Not Justified by the War on Terror

Many believe, however, that the "war on terrorism" discourse is misplaced. According to opponents of the new measures, the Attorney General is mischaracterizing the criticism. The issue is not whether critics are siding with the terrorists, as Ashcroft claims, but whether civil liberties are preserved in combating the terrorists. Although the Attorney General and Congress purport to justify the measures even under *Zadvydas*, the secrecy involved in current detentions of terrorist suspects makes it difficult to verify whether the detentions are justified. Critics believe that Congress and the Immigration Service have erroneously ignored the essence of Justice [Stephen] Breyer's *Zadvydas* opinion and have precariously focused on the mere dicta relating to terrorists. The American Civil Liberties Union (ACLU) has characterized the *Zadvydas* dicta not as an exception to the reasonably foreseeable rule, but as a question that the Court left for future consideration. According to the ACLU, the *Zadvydas* Court did not analyze the constitutionality of indefinite detention of suspected terrorists, and therefore the issue is still subject to constitutional scrutiny. In the meantime, *Zadvydas* and the basic civil liberties entitled to all persons in no way justify the powers granted to the executive branch to detain suspects in this war on terrorism.

> "Within weeks of the decision in Zadvy-
> das, INS expedited the review process
> for aliens in detention longer than 90
> days."

The *Zadvydas* Decision Has Improved U.S. Deportation Procedures

Rachel Canty

*Rachel Canty, a field operations program manager with the De-
partment of Homeland Security, holds law degree from the University of Florida and a master's in law from the University of
Miami. Here Canty outlines the swift changes in deportation
procedings after the Zadvydas decision was issued. The attorney
general, the nation's top law enforcement official, issued a memo-
randum calling on the Immigration and Naturalization Service
to improve effots to remove detained aliens. The United States
stepped up efforts to cooperate with foreign governments to get
them to accept their citizens back into their home country. In
cases where foreign governments would not cooperate, the United
States took steps suggesting it would apply punitive measures unless cooperation was forthcoming. From Canty's account, it may
be that Zadvydas did not allow many criminal aliens out on the
street, but rather gave an incentive for the immigration bureau-
cracy to send deportable aliens home more quickly.*

Rachel Canty, "The New World of Immigration Custody Determinations After *Zadvydas
v. Davis*," *Georgetown Immigration Law Journal*, vol. 18, Winter 2003–2004, pp. 467,
469–470, 481–483. Copyright © 2003–2004 Georgetown Law Journal Association. Re-
printed with permission of Georgetown Immigration Law Journal.

Prior to the United States Supreme Court's decision in *Zadvydas v. Davis*, it was not uncommon for some immigration detainees to remain in detention for significant periods of time, sometimes years following the issuance of a final order of removal in immigration proceedings. Such aliens were generally from countries that refused to accept the return of their own nationals, such as Vietnam, Laos and Cuba and were not aliens who were releasable as they were considered a flight risk or danger to the community. Then, in June 2001, the United States Supreme Court issued a decision in the case of *Zadvydas v. Davis*. In its opinion, the Court stated that although [Section] 241(a)(6) of the Immigration and [Nationality] Act (INA) generally permits the detention of aliens who have been admitted to the United States and who are under an order of removal, this detention must only be for a period of time reasonably necessary to bring about the alien's removal from the United States.

No Automatic Release

The Court went on to hold that detention of such aliens beyond the statutory removal period, for up to six months after entry of a removal order is "presumptively reasonable." After six months, if an alien can provide "good reason to believe that there is no significant likelihood of removal in the reasonably foreseeable future," the government must rebut the alien's showing, or, except in very limited circumstances, release the alien from detention. The Court specifically stated that an alien under a removal order should not automatically be released after six months if the alien has not yet been removed; "[t]o the contrary, an alien may be held in confinement until it has been determined that there is no significant likelihood of removal in the reasonably foreseeable future.". . .

In November 2001, the former INS [Immigration and Naturalization Service, now called Immigration and Customs

Enforcement (ICE)] issued interim rules amending the custody review process for aliens in detention in order to take account of the Supreme Court's ruling in *Zadvydas*. This rule added several new provisions to the already existing review process. These new provisions were designed to govern the determination as to whether there is a significant likelihood that an alien will be removed from the United States in the reasonably foreseeable future. The rule also set forth new procedures for determining whether there are special circumstances that would justify an alien's continued detention even if there were no likelihood of such removal.

At the same time, the United States Government greatly increased its interactions with foreign governments to improve the rate of removals. These efforts included the rare imposition of sanctions under [Section] 243(d) of the INA on a country, Guyana, for not issuing travel documents to their nationals in a timely manner. By statute, the imposition of such sanctions requires the Secretary of State to order consular officers in the affected country to discontinue granting immigrant visas, non-immigrant visas, or both, to citizens, subjects, nationals, and residents of such country. . . .

It should be noted that the detention of aliens in an immigration context is considered civil and non-punitive in nature. It is considered a tool, and not a goal unto itself, to be used to assist in the removal of all removable aliens from the United States. Certain classes of aliens, generally aliens with certain felony convictions, are required to be detained throughout their removal proceedings and following the issuance of a final order of removal. Aliens for whom detention during removal proceedings is not mandatory are generally detained for two purposes—ensure their appearance for immigration hearings or removal (i.e. considered to be a flight risk if released) or if the alien is considered to be a potential danger to the community. . . .

Implementing *Zadvydas*

Following the Supreme Court's decision in *Zadvydas*, the Attorney General issued a memo to the former INS, directing it to take several measures to immediately execute the decision. The memo directed the INS to draft regulations implementing the decision, and to set forth interim procedures to be used prior to the publication of the regulations. These interim procedures addressed standards for the review of alien files as well as increased international efforts to remove detained aliens expeditiously. Among the outlined interim procedures, INS was required to "immediately renew efforts to remove all aliens in post-order detention, placing special emphasis on aliens who have been detained the longest." Additionally, INS was directed to "expeditiously conclude its file review for all aliens in post order detention for 90 days or more" as well as begin to consider requests from aliens who argued that there was no significant likelihood of removal in the reasonably foreseeable future, with priority given to those aliens detained the longest.

The Attorney General memo also provided special instructions for aliens previously determined under existing procedures to pose a danger to the community. The INS was directed not to release such aliens until the case had been reviewed and there had been a determination that there was no significant likelihood of the alien's removal in the reasonably foreseeable future. The memo went on to state that if there was no likelihood of removal found, but that continued detention was deemed necessary due to "special circumstances" (left undefined in the memo) then the response to the alien should contain a description of the special circumstances. If an alien deemed a danger to the community was released, the memo provided for subjecting the alien to appropriate orders of supervision. Additionally the Attorney General memo also directed the INS to refer for prosecution appropriate cases in which, a) an alien did not cooperate with removal by refusing to make applications for travel documents or otherwise obstructed their removal, or b) an alien violated any conditions placed on their release (normally titled an order of supervision).

Pursuant to the procedures outlined in the memo, within weeks of the decision in *Zadvydas*, INS expedited the review process for aliens in detention longer than 90 days. These reviews were completed using the criteria ... which only used flight risk and danger to community in evaluating whether to release an alien. However, during the review, aliens were given a chance to submit any information they believed supported a contention that the alien's removal was not likely. INS responded in writing to any submission of information by an alien.

Getting Tough with Foreign Governments

The Attorney General memo also provided an indication of the aggressive posture to be taken by the U.S. government in relation to countries and individual aliens who did not cooperate in the removal process. The memo directed the collection of data on the removal of aliens, including data on the number of aliens who could not be removed to their country of nationality and reasons why removal was not possible. This type of data is critical to identifying which countries are not cooperating in the removal of their nationals. Under [section] 243(d) of the INA, the Secretary of State "shall order" the discontinuing of the granting of immigrant or nonimmigrant visas, or both to citizens, subjects, nationals, and residents of countries for which the Secretary of the Department of Homeland Security (the Attorney General before March 1, 2003) has determined that the government of the country "denies or reasonably delays" accepting an alien who is a citizen, subject, national or resident of that country. . . . This powerful sanction authority has rarely been used. Thus, by requesting data on non-cooperation with removals, the Attorney General memo was signaling that it was willing to take a fresh look at all available tools to effectuate the removal of aliens from the United States.

Organizations to Contact

The editors have compiled the following list of organizations concerned with the issues debated in this book. The descriptions are derived from materials provided by the organizations. All have publications or information available for interested readers. The list was compiled on the date of publication of the present volume; the information provided here may change. Be aware that many organizations take several weeks or longer to respond to inquiries, so allow as much time as possible.

American Civil Liberties Union (ACLU)
125 Broad St., 18th Floor, New York, NY   10004-2400
(800) 775-ACLU (2258)
e-mail: www.aclu.org/contact/general/index.htm
Web site: www.aclu.org

The ACLU is a national organization that works to defend the civil rights guaranteed by the U.S. Constitution. The organization's Immigrants' Rights Project advocates protections for both illegal and legal immigrants. The group publishes and distributes policy statements, pamphlets, and the semiannual newsletter *Civil Liberties Alert*.

American Immigration Law Foundation
918 F St., NW, 6th Floor, Washington, DC   20004
(202) 742-5600 • Fax: (202) 742-5619
e-mail: info@ailf.org
Web site: www.ailf.org

The American Immigration Law Foundation is dedicated to increasing public understanding of immigration law and policy and the value of immigration to American society, and to advancing fundamental fairness and due process under the law for immigrants. It is sponsored by the American Immigration Lawyers Association, and takes a generally pro-immigration attitude.

Center for Comparative Immigration Studies

University of California–San Diego, La Jolla, CA   92093
(858) 822-4447 • Fax: (858) 822-4432
e-mail: ccis@ucsd.edu
Web site: www.ccis-ucsd.org

The Center for Comparative Immigration Studies is an academically oriented institute located at the University of California, San Diego. It sponsors research on all aspects of immigration, including a major project studying the characteristics of the communities in Mexico that send a large number of migrants to the United States. The organization generally advocates more liberal immigration laws.

Center for Immigration Studies

1522 K St. NW, Suite 820, Washington, DC   20005-1202
(202) 466-8185 • fax (202) 466-8076
e-mail: center@cis.org
Web site: www.cis.org

The Center for Immigration Studies is the leading restrictionist immigration think tank. They publish a variety of reports based on original research as well as summaries of others' research, generally highlighting the costs of immigration. Their publications, most available on their Web site, also deal with the legal aspects of immigration. Web site visitors can sign up for an e-mail list notifying them of new research from the center.

The Center for Migration Studies of New York, Inc. (CMS)

27 Carmine St., New York, NY   10014
e-mail: library@cmsny.org
Web site: www.cmsny.org

The primary role of CMS of New York is to provide a forum for debating immigration issues. It publishes *International Migration Review*, a scholarly journal specializing in immigration as well as books. It also sponsors original research.

The Heritage Foundation

214 Massachusetts Ave. NE, Washington, DC 20002-4999
(202) 546-4400 • fax: (202) 546-0904
e-mail: info@heritage.org
Web site: www.heritage.org

The Heritage Foundation is a conservative public-policy research institute dedicated to free-market principles, individual
liberty, and limited government. It has recently turned its attention to immigration, for example, publishing an analysis of
the cost of amnesty for illegal aliens ("Amnesty Will Cost
United States Taxpayers at Least $2.6 Trillion," by Robert Rec-
tor, June 6, 2007). It also produces the quarterly journal *Policy
Review* and the bimonthly newsletter *Heritage Today* as well as
numerous books and papers.

National Council of La Raza

Raul Yzaguirre Building, 1126 16th St., NW
Washington, DC 20036
(202) 785-1670 • Fax (202) 776-1792
email: comments@nclr.org
Web site: www.nclr.org

The National Council of La Raza is the nation's largest group
promoting the interests of Hispanic Americans. As such it focuses much effort on protecting the rights of immigrants. The
attorneys of the council's local affiliates have been instrumen-
tal in such cases as *Plyler v. Doe*. It also advocates increased
participation of Latinos in the political process with projects
to help recent immigrants obtain citizenship, among other
programs.

National Immigration Forum

50 F St. NW, Suite 300, Washington, DC 20001
(202) 347-0040 • fax: (202) 347-0058
email: media@immigrationforum.org
Web site: www.immigrationforum.org

With a Web site that proclaims that "Immigrants are America"
and states that the group is dedicated to "upholding America's
tradition as a nation of immigrants," the National Immigra-

tion Forum is squarely on the side of immigrants legal and illegal. The group publishes downloadable "backgrounders" on immigration issues (available on the Web site) as well as frequent updates highlighting current issues in immigration law.

Urban Institute

2100 M St., NW, Washington, DC   20037
(202) 833-7200
Web site: www.urban.org

The Urban Institute advocates for the urban poor in America. Since the 1980s, the group's Immigration Studies program has researched the impact of immigration on America's cities and workforce. Their research addresses immigrants' contributions to the U.S. economy and tax base as well as lower-paid immigrants' needs for work supports such as tax credits, health insurance, and child care.

For Further Research

Books

T. Alexander Aleinikoff and Douglas B. Klusmeyer, eds., *From Migrants to Citizens: Membership in a Changing World.* Washington, DC: Carnegie Endowment for International Peace, 2000.

Richard A. Boswell, *Immigration and Nationality Law: Cases and Materials.* 3rd ed. Durham, NC: Carolina Academic Press, 2000.

Steven A. Camarota and Center for Immigration Studies, *The Open Door: How Militant Islamic Terrorists Entered and Remained in the United States, 1993–2001.* Washington, DC: Center for Immigration Studies, 2002.

Gabriel J. Chin, Victor C. Romero, and Michael A. Scaperlanda, eds., *Immigration and the Constitution.* New York: Garland, 2002.

Roger Daniels and Otis L. Graham, *Debating American Immigration, 1882–Present.* Lanham, MD: Rowman & Littlefield, 2001.

Mark Dow, *American Gulag: Inside U.S. Immigration Prisons.* Berkeley: University of California Press, 2004.

John Fonte and Center for Immigration Studies, *Dual Allegiance: A Challenge to Immigration Reform and Patriotic Assimilation.* Washington, DC: Center for Immigration Studies, 2005.

Elspeth Guild and Anneliese Baldaccini, eds., *Terrorism and the Foreigner. A Decade of Tension Around the Rule of Law in Europe.* Boston: Martinus Nijhoff, 2007.

Theodore B. Gunderson, *Immigration Policy in Turmoil.* Huntington, NY: Nova Science, 2002.

Jeremy Harding, *The Uninvited: Refugees at the Rich Man's Gate*. London: Profile, 2000.

Kevin R. Johnson, *The "Huddled Masses" Myth: Immigration and Civil Rights*. Philadelphia: Temple University Press, 2004.

Daniel Kanstroom, *Deportatton Nation: Outsiders in American History*. Cambridge, MA: Harvard University Press, 2007.

Lon Kurashige and Alice Yang Murray, eds., *Major Problems in Asian American History: Documents and Essays*. Boston: Houghton Mifflin, 2003.

Ira J. Kurzban, *Kurzban's Immigration Law Sourcebook: A Comprehensive Outline and Reference Tool*. 10th ed. Washington, DC: American Immigration Law Foundation, 2006.

Estelle T. Lau, *Paper Families: Identity, Immigration Administration, and Chinese Exclusion*. Durham, NC: Duke University Press, 2006.

James P. Lynch and Rita J. Simon, *Immigration the World Over: Statutes, Policies, and Practices*. Lanham, MD: Rowman & Littlefield, 2003.

Douglas S. Massey and Cato Institute, *Backfire at the Border: Why Enforcement Without Legalization Cannot Stop Illegal Immigration*. Washington, DC: Cato Institute, 2005.

Douglas S. Massey, Jorge Durand, and Nolan J. Malone, *Beyond Smoke and Mirrors: Mexican Immigration in an Era of Economic Integration*. New York: Russell Sage Foundation, 2002.

Cesar Muñoz Acebes, *Presumption of Guilt: Human Rights Abuses of Post–September 11 Detainees*. New York: Human Rights Watch, 2002.

Mae M. Ngai, *Impossible Subjects: Illegal Aliens and the Making of Modern America*. Princeton, NJ: Princeton University Press, 2004.

John S.W. Park, *Elusive Citizenship: Immigration, Asian Americans, and the Paradox of Civil Rights*. New York: New York University Press, 2004.

Victor C. Romero, *Alienated: Immigrant Rights, the Constitution, and Equality in America*. New York: New York University Press, 2005.

Nikolai Wenzel, *America's Other Border Patrol: The State Department's Consular Corps and Its Role in U.S. Immigration*. Washington, DC: Center for Immigration Studies, 2000.

Periodicals

Kerry Abrams, "Polygamy, Prostitution, and the Federalization of Immigration Law," *Columbia Law Review*, April 2005.

Victoria Cook Capitaine, "Life in Prison Without a Trial: The Indefinite Detention of Immigrants in the United States," *Texas Law Review*, February 2001.

Adam B. Cox, "Citizenship, Standing, and Immigration Law," *California Law Review*, March 2004.

Carole Boyce Davies, "Deportable Subjects: U.S. Immigration Laws and the Criminalizing of Communism," *South Atlantic Quarterly*, Fall 2001.

Economist "Dreaming of the Other Side of the Wire," March 12, 2005.

Economist "Rolling up the Welcome Mat," February 12, 2005.

Brian Grow and Dan Beucke, "Rising Numbers, Rising Resistance," *Business Week*, October 10, 2005.

Victor Davis Hanson, "Mexifornia, Five Years Later," *City Journal* Winter 2007.

Robin Jacobson, "Characterizing Consent: Race, Citizenship, and the New Restrictionists," *Political Research Quarterly*, December 2006.

Tamar Jacoby, "Should the U.S. End Birthright Citizenship?," *New York Times Upfront*, April 3, 2006.

Kevin R. Johnson and Bill Ong Hing, "National Identity in a Multicultural Nation: The Challenge of Immigration Law and Immigrants," *Michigan Law Review*, May 2005.

Mark Krikorian, "Giving Enforcement a Chance," *National Review*, January 1, 2006.

———, "Not So Realistic" (Cover Story), *National Review*, September 12, 2005.

Trevor Morrison, "The Supreme Court and Immigration Law: A New Commitment to Avoiding Hard Constitutional Questions?" findlaw.com, July 31, 2001.

National Review "Not Amnesty but Attrition," March 22, 2004.

New Republic "Border Crossing," July 30, 2001.

George Putnam, "One Reporter's Opinion: Immigration Insanity," Newsmax.com, May 16, 2004.

Raul Reyes, "Kids of Illegal Aliens Face Bully Treatment," *USA Today*, November 25, 2005.

Michael S. Teitelbaum, "Immigration: The Opinion Gap," *Christian Science Monitor*, April 17, 2006.

Jennifer Welch, "Defending Against Deportation: Equipping Public Defenders to Represent Noncitizens Effectively," *California Law Review*, March 2004.

Internet Sources

Immigration Law Professors Blog (http://lawprofessors
.typepad.com/immigration). This frequently updated site is
a great source for current news on immigration issues.
The three University of California at Davis Immigration
law professors who run the site—Kevin R. Johnson, Bill
O. Hing, and Jennifer Chacón—are on the side of large-
scale immigration. The site, however, features many links
to news stories that will be of interest to people on all
sides of the debate.

The Oyez Project (www.oyez.org). This Web site is a multi-
media collection focused exclusively on the Supreme
Court. Sound recordings of oral arguments in front of the
Court are available, as is a recording of the famous
"oyez, oyez, oyez" that opens each Court session. The
site also features biographies of the justices and a virtual
tour of the Supreme Court building.

Vdare.Com (www.vdare.com). Named after Virginia Dare,
the first English child born in the New World, the controversial Vdare.com Web site is unabashedly anti-mass immigration. Writers in its "collective" range from liberal
Democrats to (moderate) white nationalists. In keeping
with this diversity, the site addresses everything from
immigration-driven population growth to what they see as
pro-immigration media bias.

Index

A

al-Arian, Sami, 17
Aliens. *See* Immigrants
Alito, Samuel, 48–49, 50
Aljets, Borrero v., 146
American Civil Liberties Union (ACLU), 154
American taxpayers, *Plyler* decision and, 118–124
Anti-immigration policies, 115–116
Arroyave, N. Alejandra, 149
Ashcroft, John, 153
Assimilation, attempts at, 36

B

Balkin, Jack M., 52
Baumgartner v. United States, 73
Bica, De Canas v., 102–103
Bingham, John A., 44
Birthright citizenship
    controversy over, 14–16, 48–52
    court decisions opposing, 44–45
    Court's opinion on, 20–28
    dissenting opinion on, 29–35
    racial aspect of debate on, 37–40
See also United States v. Wong Kim Ark (1898)
Board of Education, Brown v., 91–92, 109
Borrero v. Aljets, 146
Bosniak, Linda, 108
Brennan, Howard L., 50

Brennan, William, 86, 88, 106, 119–123
Breyer, Stephen, 126–127, 128, 154
Brown v. Board of Education (1954), 91–92, 109
Burger, Warren, 97, 123–124
Bush, George W., 50, 110

C

Canty, Rachel, 155
Children
    deserve special protection, 89–100
    Plyler decision ignores needs of American, 118–124
    of temporary residents, 31–32
Children of illegal immigrants
    denying education to, is not unconstitutional, 97–104
    right to education of, 14–16, 20–21, 84–96
China, treaties between U.S. and, 33–34
Chinese Exclusion Acts, 20, 37–38
Chinese immigrants, prejudice against, 37–38
Chinese law, nationality changes and, 29–30
Citizenship
    common law and, 24–25
    Constitution on, 23–24
    controversy over, in light of war on terror, 70–72
    eligibility for, 14–16
    exceptions to, at birth, 26–27
    as heritage, 30–31
    revocation of, 16, 72–76
    sources of, 27–28

two-class system of, 74–75, 82–83

See also Birthright citizenship; Naturalization

Civil rights, 16–17, 149–154

Coke, Edward, 26

College education, 110

Common law, 23–25, 31–32

Communist Party

membership in, can be grounds for deportation, 64–69

membership in, is not grounds for deportation, 56–63

Scheniderman case and, 16, 54, 77–80, 83

Congressional powers, usurpation of, 123–124

Constitution

on citizenship, 23–24

communism is not compatible with, 68–69

does not guarantee right to education, 97–104

principles of, and naturalization, 78–81

rights guaranteed by, 62–63

Criminal aliens

cannot be detained indefinitely, 128–135

danger posed by, 138–139, 141–148

deportation of, 126–127

do not have to be released, 136–142

Critical race theory, 112–117

D

Davis, Zadvydas v. See Zadvydas v. Davis (2001)

De Canas v. Bica, 102–103

Deal, Nathan, 49–50

Denationalization, 72–73

Denaturalization, 72–73, 75–76, 80–83

Deportation

affect of *Zadvydas* decision on, 155–160

of criminal aliens, 126–127

of naturalized citizens, is not allowed, 56–63

political opinions can be grounds for, 64–69

requires compelling evidence, 83–84

Detention review process, 156–157

Development, Relief, and Education for Alien Minors (DREAM) Act, 110

Dissent, 14, 16–17

Doe, Plyler v. See Plyler v. Doe (1982)

Dole, Robert, 109

Douglas, William O., 65, 82

Dred Scott case (1857), 39

Due Process Clause, 129–130

E

Eastman, John C., 51

Economics, of illegal immigration, 113–114

Education

Court's decision on illegal immigrant children's right to, 88–96

debate over, for children of illegal immigrants, 86–87

denial of, to illegal immigrants, in California, 109, 115

denying to, illegal immigrants is not unconstitutional, 97–104 illegal immigrant children do not hurt quality of, 94–95, 114–115

importance of, 90–92

is not a fundamental right, 100–101

Election politics, 109–110

Elk v. Wilkins (1884), 45, 51

English common law, 24–25, 31–32

Equal Protection Clause, 91, 99, 101, 107–108, 119–121

Erler, Edward, 16

Esposito, John, 17

Executive branch, foreign policy and, 133–135, 137

Expatriation, 72–73

F

Fahy, Charles, 80

Fifteenth Amendment, 31

Fifth Amendment, 107, 129–130

First Amendment, 63, 81–82

Fong Yue Ting v. U.S., 35

Fontana, David, 77

Foreign policy decisions, of executive branch, 133–135, 137

Foreign powers, allegiance to, 30, 47

Foreigners, expulsion of, 30–31

Fourteenth Amendment
citizenship clause in, 14–16, 20, 25–27, 30–32, 39, 41, 45–47

Court's interpretation of, 49–51

Equal Protection Clause of, 91, 99, 101, 107–108, 119–121

Frankfurter, Felix, 74, 75–76, 82

Free speech rights, 55, 81–82

Freedom of thought, 62–63

Fuller, Melville, 21, 29, 46

G

Gallegly Amendment, 109–110, 116

Garcia, R. J., 112

Gompers, Samuel, 37–39

Graham v. Richardson, 106

Gray, Horace, 20–21, 22, 42

Guantanamo Bay prisoners, 146–147

H

Habeas corpus, 126–127, 146–147

Happersett, Minor v. (1874), 46

Hatch, Orrin, 110

Ho, James C., 15

Holland, Rosales-Garcia v., 145–146

Holmes, Oliver Wendell, 63

Hooker, Charles H., 70

Howard, Jacob M., 42, 43, 45, 46

Hughes, Charles E., 58, 59

I

Illegal immigrant children
denying education to, is not unconstitutional, 97–104

denying education to, is racially biased, 111–117

right of education for, 14–16, 20–21, 86–96

treatment of, 106

Illegal immigrants
exclusion of, from welfare programs, 103–104

numbers of, 14

public opinion in, 50

racial prejudice toward, 111–117

as suspect class, 92–93, 101

Wong Kim Ark case and,
51–52
Illegal immigration
denial of education does not
deter, 93–94
economics of, 113–114
Illegal Immigration and Immigrant Responsibility Act (1996),
109, 116
Illiteracy, 91, 107
Immigrants
Chinese, 37–38
civil rights of, 16–17, 149–154
history of detention of, 132–
133
Latino, 39–40
Mexican, 39–40, 111–117
Muslim, 14, 17
naturalization of, 14–16
numbers of, 14
post-9/11 legislation affecting,
149–154
power to detain, 151–152
prejudice against, 37–40, 111–
117
See also Criminal aliens; Illegal
Immigration
controversy over, 14, 48–52
election politics and, 109–110
as federal concern, 107–108
national security and, 16–17
racial prejudice and, 111–117
treaties governing, 33–34, 112
See also Illegal immigration
Immigration and Customs Enforcement (ICE), 156–157
Immigration and Nationality Act
(INA), 137–138, 152
Immigration and Naturalization
Service (INS)
detainment by, 128–135, 150

implementation of *Zadvydas*
by, 158–159
Indefinite detention
affect of *Zadvydas* decision
on, 155–160
is not permitted, 128–135
post-9/11 legislation on, 149–
154
should be permitted, 136–142
Individual rights
Plyler decision and, 105–110
post-9/11 legislation affecting, 149–154
Islamic organizations, 14, 17

J

Judicial review, 124, 133–134

K

Kennedy, Anthony, 127, 136, 144–
145, 147

L

Latino immigrants, discrimination
against, 39–40
Legislative intent, *Wong Kim Ark*
case ignores, 41–47

M

Ma, Kim Ho, 126, 129, 135, 144
Madison, P.A., 41
Medicaid, 103–104
Medicare, 103–104
Mexican immigrants, discrimina-
tion against, 39–40, 111–117
Minor v. Happersett (1874), 46
Murphy, Frank, 56, 75, 81–82
Muslim immigrants, 14, 17

N

National Act (1940), 74
National security
    immigration and, 16–17
    post-9/11/ legislation affect-
        ing, 149–154
    relevance of *Schneiderman*
        case to, 70–76
    Zadvydas decision threatens,
        143–148
Native Americans, citizenship of,
    46–47
Naturalization
    of immigrants, 14–16, 27
    as privilege, 60–62
    rules governing, 60–62, 64–65
    terms of, 78–79
Naturalized citizens
    can be deported, for political
        opinions, 64–69
    civil rights of, 16–17, 54–55
    dissent by, is not grounds for
        deportation, 56–63
    equality for, 74–75
    loyalty issues with, 77–84
Nazis, 73–74

O

Olivas, Michael A., 105

P

Plyler v. Doe (1982)
    case overview, 86–87
    Court's decision in, 88–96
    dissenting opinion in, 97–104
    ignored needs of American
        taxpayers, 118–124
    importance of, for individual
        rights, 105–110
    is blow to racial prejudice,
        111–117

political aspects of, 109–110
Political opinions
    can be grounds for deporta-
        tion, 64–69
    extreme, are not grounds for
        deportation, 56–63
    upholding of right to, by
        Court, 54–55
Politics, immigration and, 109–
    110
Powell, Lewis, 101
Prejudice, against immigrants,
    37–38, 111–117
Proposition 187, 109, 115
Public education. *See* Education

R

Racial aspects
    of birthright citizenship de-
        bate, 37–40
    of *Plyer* decision, 111–117
Reagan, Ronald, 123
Repatriation, 139–141
Reyes, Raul, 15
Richardson, Graham v., 106
Rincón, Alejandra, 111
Roberts, Owen, 82
Roos, Peter, 110
Rosales-Garcia v. Holland, 145–146
Rutledge, Wiley, 82

S

Sandler, Michael, 48
Sanford, Scott v. (1857), 25
Schneiderman, United States v.
    (1943). *See United States v.*
    Schneiderman
Schuck, Peter, 108
Schumer, Charles E., 49, 50
Scott v. Sanford (1857), 25

Security
  concerns over, 14
  immigration and, 16–17
  See also National security
September 11, 2001, security concerns after, 14
Sheridan, Christopher, 143
Slaughterhouse cases, 44–45
Smith, William French, 123
Social welfare programs, exclusion of illegal immigrants from, 103–104
States
  cannot deny illegal immigrant children education, 88–96
  have right to deny illegal immigrant children education, 97–104
  immigration and, 107–108
Stevens, John Paul, 42
Stone, Harlan Fiske, 64, 82–83
Sutherland, Howard, 118

T

Taney, Roger, 25
Temporary residents, children of, 31–32
Terrorism threat
  concern about, 14
  relevance of *Schneiderman* case to, 70–76
  See also War on terror
Terrorists, *Zadvydas* decision allows, to live in U.S., 143–148
Thought, freedom of, 62–63
Treaties, governing immigration, 33–34, 112
Treaty of Guadalupe Hidalgo, 112
Trumbull, Lyman, 42, 43–44, 45

U

Undeportable aliens
  cannot be detained indefinitely, 128–135
  civil rights of, 126–127
  do not have to be released, 136–142
Undocumented aliens. *See* Illegal immigrants
United States
  treaties between China and, 33–34
  Zadvydas decision allows terrorist to live in, 143–148
United States, Baumgartner v., 73
United States v. Schneiderman (1943)
  case overview, 54–55
  Court's opinion in, 56–63
  dissenting opinion in, 64–69
  government's case in, 80–81
  implications of, 14, 16–17
  loyalty issues in, 77–84
  renewed relevance of, in war on terror, 70–76
  as test case, 79–80
United States v. Wong Kim Ark (1894)
  arguments in, 38–39
  case overview, 20–21
  controversy over, 48–52
  dissenting opinion in, 29–35
  ignores legislative intent, 41–47
  illegal immigration and, 51–52
  implications of, 14–16
  is milestone in treating Americans fairly, 36–40
  majority decision in, 22–28
U.S. Constitution. *See* Constitution
U.S. government, dissent against, 14, 16–17

USA PATRIOT Act, 151–152

W

War on terror
  detention of aliens and, 149–154
  relevance of *Schneiderman* case to, 70–76
Washington Legal Foundation (WLF), 143–144
Welfare programs, exclusion of illegal immigrants from, 103–104
Wilkins, Elk v. (1884), 45, 51
Willkie, Wendell, 54, 81
Wilson, Pete, 109
Wong Kim Ark, United States v. (1894), *See United States v. Wong Kim Ark*

Wu, Frank, 36

Z

Zadvydas, Kestutis, 126, 129–130, 134
Zadvydas v. Davis (2001)
  allows potential terrorist to live in U.S., 143–148
  case overview, 126–127
  Court's decision in, 128–135
  dissenting opinion in, 136–142
  has improved deportation procedures, 155–160
  implementation of, 158–159
  post-9/11/ legislation has invalidated, 149–154